Cyprus

Front cover: The Sanctuary of Apollo
Hylates/Ylatis
Right: Aphrodite in the Cyprus Museum

TOP 10 ATTRACTIONS

Panagia tou Araka. One of the island's most celebrated frescoed churches, in Lagoudera village. See page 68.

Keryneia. The medieval harbour is the most picturesque in Cyprus. See page 8

Cyprus Museum. A must-see in Nicosia, housing the Island's finest collection of archaeological artefacts. See page 30.

Buffavento. Highest of three Lusignan castles in the Pentadaktylos range, this has superb views over half the island. See page 80.

Sunderland
City Council

This book is due for return to the library indicated on or before the last date entered below. Overdue charges at the current rate will be charged if the book is returned after that date.

You can renew your items by telephoning the 24-hour renewals service on 0191 5250111, or visit the library website at **www.sunderland.gov.uk/libraries**

Agia Napa. Blonde-sand beaches and excellent hotels have made this one of the Island's top destinations. See page 50.

Famagusta. The old town, wrapped in impressive Venetian fortifications, holds many Gothic churches now used as mosques. See page 83.

Kato Pafos. Some of the finest Roman mosaics in the east Mediterranean grace this resort. See page 69.

Karpaz Peninsula. Byzantine monuments, the island's best seafood and superb, deserted beaches make this remote area a winner. See page 86.

Agios Neofytos Monastery. The highlight here is the frescoed, rock-cut hermitage. See page 76.

Kourion. The ancient clifftop city, one of Cyprus' archaeological highlights, offers mosaics and a restored temple. See page 56.

A PERFECT TOUR

Day 1   Larnaka

Arrive at Larnaka Airport, pick up your hire car, head into town for the Pierides and Archaeological museums. Lunch at a restaurant along Piyale Paşa, booking a dive for tomorrow over the *Zenobia* wreck. Drive west to accommodation in Tochni or Kalavasos. Dinner at nearby Zygi, or perhaps Limassol.

Days 4   Keryneia

Take your car across at Agios Dometios/Metehan and reach Keryneia waterfront in time for lunch. Afterwards, head up to Bellapais/Beylerbeyi with its Gothic abbey. Check into accommodation in Keryneia or Bellapais.

Day 3   Nicosia

Head early to Nicosia; visit the Cyprus and Byzantine museums. Later, explore the Mevlevî Tekke and the Selimiye Camii in North Nicosia. Return to the southern sector for dinner in the old town.

Day 5   Karpasia

Next day, head east to Kantara Castle, gateway to Karpasia. Lunch at a recommended local fish taverna, stopping afterwards at Agias Trias basilica with its fine mosaics. Enjoy a late afternoon swim at Nangomi/Golden Beach, then overnight at a recommended lodging in Dipkarpaz (Rizokarpaso). Watch the sunset from Agios Filon/Ayfilon cove.

Day 2   Limassol

Return to Larnaka for a mid-morning dive of the *Zenobia*. Spend the middle of the day in Limassol, at the Cyprus Medieval Museum, and then lunch in the old quarter. Head to Kourion for a late afternoon visit, before dinner.

OF CYPRUS

Day 7 — Troödos painted churches

Start with Agios Nikolaos tis Stegis beside Kakopetria, then move to the Marathassa valley for Agios Lambadistis monastery and early lunch in Kalopanagiotis. Assuming a long spring day, spend the afternoon hiking the Madari loop trail (3 hours). Alternatively, visit the spectacular church of Panagia tou Araka nearby. Change base to Pano Platres.

Day 10 — Homeward

Return to Larnaka Airport, or preferably Pafos Airport, for flight home.

Day 6 — Three towns

Get an early start towards ancient Salamis, and then Famagusta to view the walls and Gothic mosque, before lunch at Gingko. Use fast roads west to the Kato Zodeia-Astromeritis border crossing, stopping at Galata to view its frescoed churches, then arriving at old Kakopetria for an overnight and dinner at Tziellari.

Day 8 — To Pafos

Leave Pano Platres via a Limassol foothill winery, then change valleys for lunch at Ariadni's outside Vasa. A lovely route leads quickly downhill, via Koulkia and Palaia Paphos, to Pafos, where you overnight. Dinner at Seven St Georges Taverna.

Day 9 — Around Pafos

Spend the morning at the world-class Pafos Mosaics, then the hermitage of St Neophytos. After lunch at Laona in Ktima marketplace, spend the afternoon at the turtle beach of Lara. Overnight as previous day; dinner at Imogen's in Kathikas.

CONTENTS

INTRODUCTION

Cyprus rose to prominence in antiquity from its copper deposits – indeed the island's name is the basis for the Latin word for the metal (cuprum). In modern times, Cyprus' greatest natural resource is sunshine, over 300 days of it per year. Yet 'Aphrodite's Island' has often been careless with the coastline that puts all that sunshine to good use. Many resorts are large and over-developed, with little historical or cultural character, and the battle to preserve the remaining unspoiled coastline is being closely fought. Delve inland for a greater appreciation of this island: countless ancient sites, sleepy villages, frescoed country churches, terraced hillside vineyards and rugged mountain ranges await you. The layers of a long and tangled history, from Stone Age peoples, through Greeks, Phoenicians, Persians, Romans, Byzantines, Crusaders, Venetians, Genoese, Ottomans and British, are there to be seen and felt.

Some of your finest memories are likely to be of a remarkably friendly and hospitable people – both Greek-Cypriot and Turkish-Cypriot – despite their turbulent and traumatic recent history. This is, after all, an island that was invaded by Turkey and split in two in 1974. Within weeks, some 180,000 Greek Cypriots were forced to flee to the south of the island, becoming refugees in their own country. Within a year, around 44,000 Turkish Cypriots had moved north. The island is still divided today, though since 2003 there has been greater freedom of movement across the de facto border.

Although it's simple to visit the North (which only Turkey recognises as a separate republic), most travellers still choose the Greek-Cypriot South. But for those who do cross the ceasefire line that separates the two parts of the island, the North

The remains of a Byzantine basilica at Kourion

The grape harvest

offers the best Lusignan and Venetian monuments, some excellent beaches and appealingly empty landscapes.

An Easy-Going People

Through all the turmoil, the Cypriots have managed to retain a sunny, relaxed disposition. Ask a couple harvesting grapes if you can take their photo, and they will not only strike a happy pose, but also gather a large bag of grapes for you to take home. Compliment a chef on the quality of his *sheftaliá* at a taverna and chat to him about village life, and it's not impossible he will insist that lunch is on the house. It is rare that a visitor leaves Cyprus without some tale of the people's generosity.

It is not a mere marketing gimmick that at the end of a meal, coffee and a liqueur (either citrus-flavoured or the clear spirit *zivania*) is provided on the house. You don't have to go to the most remote mountain village for such hospitality, but it is also true that you are much less likely to find this warmth in the more obviously tourist-oriented watering holes.

This widespread cheerfulness is coupled with a dignity that shuns expansive Latin gestures. The British like to think that their presence on the island has been at least partly responsible, but the courtesy of Cypriots in general seems to be a more deeply ingrained quality.

Troubled Relations

A more sombre note is struck when the matter of the divided island is raised. Greek-Cypriot refugees from the North react more with melancholy than anger. Nostalgically, restaurants and shops in Larnaka or Limassol may bear the names of their lost homes in Famagusta, Keryneia or Bellapais. Turkish-Cypriot refugees from the South are usually less nostalgic, and less inclined to consider going back to live should matters ever permit this – though by preference they now work, educate their children and seek health care in the South. The recent changes that brought Greek and Turkish Cypriots into closer contact with each other have taken the edge off some resentments, but others linger…

Because of its geographical position, Cyprus has been beset by unwelcome visitors throughout its history. Apart from

The Lie of the Land

Tucked into the extreme eastern corner of the Mediterranean between Turkish Anatolia and Syria, Cyprus is the Mediterranean's third largest island, after Sicily and Sardinia. Its land surface of 9,251 sq km (3,572 sq miles) sandwiches the broad Mesaoria Plain between two chains of mountains – the Pentadaktylos range in the northeast and the Troödos in the southwest. Three major rivers, which run dry in summer, originate in the Troödos Mountains: the Pediaios, flowing east to Famagusta Bay; the Kargotis, north to Morfou Bay; and the Kouris, south to Episkopi. The highest peak is Mt Olympos, at 1,952m (6,403ft).

Population: Almost 1 million in the South, including 200,000 foreign residents; 200,000 in the North, including 80,000 post-1974 Turkish settlers.

Capital: Nicosia (Lefkosia/Lefkoşa): 240,000 in the Greek-Cypriot sector; 70,000 in the Turkish-Cypriot sector.

Major cities: South: Limassol (Lemesos; 190,000), Larnaka (84,000), Pafos (60,000). North: Famagusta (Ammochostos/Gazimağusa; 43,000), Morfou (Güzelyurt; 15,000), Keryneia (Girne; 65,000).

Pano Lefkara in the Troödos foothills

attracting conquerors from Phoenicia, Egypt, Persia, Greece and Anatolia, Cyprus was easy prey for Latin crusaders and the Venetian republic, and was even a pawn in the last days of the British Empire.

The Island's Attractions

For today's visitors, the traces of the past are a compelling reason for coming. There are ancient Greek and Roman ruins at Kourion and Salamis, splendid Roman mosaics at Pafos, Crusader castles at Kolossi and atop the Pentadakylos Mountains, and Byzantine monasteries and churches of the Troödos Mountains.

Cyprus is a country of great natural beauty. While the most popular resort beaches cater for holidaymakers happy to lie baking in serried ranks, the coastline, particularly along the Akamas and Karpaz peninsulas, has enough rugged cliffs and surf-beaten coves to appeal to the romantic individualist or rugged off-road biker. Inland, the Troödos Mountains are a spectacularly verdant realm of hairpin curves and restored forest. Sprinkled like forgotten gems in the landscape are tiny Byzantine churches, known only to their parishioners for centuries. Today, many of these are protected by Unesco and no visit to Cyprus is complete without visiting several of them.

Inland villages untouched by tourism nestle among olive groves or citrus orchards, while goats and sheep scamper among forgotten medieval ruins. Vineyards climb the sunny hillsides, cypress trees frame a somnolent abbey or the skeleton of an abandoned fortress, and rural Cypriot life continues at a gentle pace.

Name Games

Authorities in both southern and northern Cyprus have engaged in wholesale campaigns of renaming places in recent decades, for similar nationalistic motivations. In 1994, the decades-old British system of transliterating Greek into the Latin alphabet – which had the major advantage of giving a reasonable phonetic pronunciation, in Cypriot dialect, of the place concerned – was replaced, by extreme nationalists in two ministries, with a new 'politically correct' scheme combining the worst features of two systems used by classicists. Thus Nicosia became Lefkosia; Larnaca, Larnaka; Paphos, Pafos; Ayia Napa, Agia Napa, and so on. The new scheme, though mandatory in official use and overseas cartography, remains deeply unpopular – most businesses, tour operators and NGOs opt out of it. In the North, since the Turkish incursion, all Greek place-names have been replaced by Turkish ones, often invented, and often ignoring perfectly good Ottoman versions of town-names long used by Turkish Cypriots. In this guide, we cite the new 'approved' nomenclature first, followed by the 'old-style' name, if significantly different, in brackets for places in the South; for the North, we cite the new Greek Cypriot nomenclature first, followed by the Turkish renaming in brackets.

A BRIEF HISTORY

The first humans on Cyprus were nomads and hunters rather than permanently settled groups. Flint tools discovered offshore from the Akamas Peninsula and on Nissi Beach at Agia Napa prove that seafarers landed on Cyprus in about 10,000 BC. The bones of indigenous pygmy hippopotamuses and pygmy elephants (both now extinct) eaten by the mariners were also found. Tools and butchered animal bones found in a coastal cave at Akrotiri date from about 9000 BC. The earliest traces of permanent settlers date from about 8000 BC, the most notable being the stone beehive-shaped dwellings at the tip of the Karpaz Peninsula and at the inland sites of Choirokoitia (Khirokitía) and Tenta (Ténda).

By 3500 BC, copper was being mined in the Troödos foothills and Cyprus began to prosper as a trading centre, with goods arriving from Asia, Egypt, Crete, the Peloponnese and the Aegean islands in exchange for Cypriot pottery, copperware and opium. After 1600 BC, fortresses appear, which suggests a period of insecurity and outside threats.

Greeks, Persians and Romans

Climactic and demographic upheaval in the Peloponnese drove Mycenaean Greeks east across the Mediterranean, and some settled in Cyprus. Around 1200 BC, they established city-kingdoms at Enkomi/Alasia Salamis (near modern Famagusta), Marion (near Polis), Tamassos, Kition (now Larnaka), Kourion, Palaia Pafos (modern Kouklia), Soloi and Lapethos. The island acquired the predominantly Greek identity it was never entirely to relinquish.

As the Persian Empire spread across the eastern Mediterranean in the 6th century BC, Cyprus, along with other Greek islands, was annexed. In 499 BC it joined the Ionian Greek revolt but, after heroic resistance, notably during the sieges of Soloi and Palaia Pafos, was crushed by the Persians the next year.

In 333 BC, Alexander the Great ended Persian dominance in the eastern Mediterranean and placed Cyprus under Macedonian rule. After his death in 323 BC, his generals fought over the succession, flattening many Cypriot cities in the process. By 294 BC, Ptolemy I emerged the victor, the city-kingdoms disappeared and Cyprus became part of Hellenistic Egypt. The Ptolemies ruled for 250 years until the Romans annexed it in 58 BC to their province of Cilicia (southern Turkey).

In 47 BC, Julius Caesar made a present of Cyprus to Cleopatra, the last Ptolemaic ruler. After her suicide, Augustus took it back for the Romans and let King Herod of Judaea farm out the Cypriot copper mines to Jewish entrepreneurs.

Original mosaic of Leda and the Swan at Kouklia

The Byzantine Era

Despite the apostle Paul's mission to Cyprus in AD 45, most islanders continued to be devoutly pagan, though not Jewish – all Jews were expelled by Emperor Hadrian after a bloody revolt in AD 116. Only during the 4th century, as Christianity spread to the Roman leadership, did churches and monasteries multiply across Cyprus. In AD 330, the mother of Roman emperor Constantine,

Helena, supposedly visited the island and founded the great Stavrovouni Monastery.

In 488, when the relics of Barnabas (Paul's evangelising companion) were miraculously found, the Church of Cyprus became autonomous, subject only to Constantinople, and not nearby Antioch or Jerusalem. The archbishop of Cyprus could carry a royal sceptre rather than a pastoral staff, wear a cloak of imperial purple and sign his name in imperial red ink – rights that the archbishops retain to this day.

With the Byzantine Empire weakened by war against Persia, the Arabs took the opportunity to attack Cyprus in 649 with a fleet of 1,500 ships. Salamis (now Constantia) was left in such ruins that it never recovered; raiding continued until an approaching Byzantine fleet prompted retreat.

Four years later, in a move that foreshadowed events of the 20th century, the Arabs staged a second invasion and left a garrison of 12,000 men, encouraging Muslim civilian immigration. The Byzantines and the Caliphate subsequently agreed to demilitarise Cyprus and also to share tax revenues. Over the next 300 years, Muslims and Christians engaged in offshore battles, but lived side by side.

Asset strippers

Although King Richard the Lionheart deposed the 'emperor' Komnenos, he pillaged the island to pay for his onward expedition to the Holy Land, and got 40 percent of the purchase price for Cyprus up front from the Knights Templar. They in turn had to raise the balance with confiscatory taxation, which prompted a local rebellion.

The Crusades and the Lusignans

During the Crusades, Cyprus became a key strategic post for Byzantine interests in Syria and Palestine. The governor organised protection for pilgrims to the Holy Land and supervised the rebuilding of Jerusalem's Church of the Holy Sepulchre and fortifications for its Christian Quarter. The invasion of Seljuk Turks in Anatolia and the Levant after 1071 threatened communications with Constantinople, but Cyprus was still able to supply soldiers of the First Crusade in 1097 and even provided refuge for defeated Muslim princes.

New trade developed with Venice and the young Crusader states on the mainland. However, the Seljuks' domination of Anatolia after 1176 isolated Cyprus from the Byzantine government. Isaac Komnenos, a junior member of the imperial family, declared himself 'Emperor' of Cyprus in 1184.

A Stavrovouni mosaic depicts Byzantine-era Christianity

Deliverance from his greedy, brutal rule came in the form of England's King Richard the Lionheart, who anchored at Limassol en route to the Third Crusade. After a brief campaign, he defeated and imprisoned Komnenos, then promptly sold the island to the Knights Templar. Their greed prompted another revolt which they could not quell, and the island returned briefly to Richard's suzerainty before being acquired by Guy de Lusignan, a French former king of Jerusalem. Lusignan recreated the lost feudal world of Palestine, parcelling out Cyprus' farmland to over 500 supporters, and reducing native Cypriots to serfdom. In 1260, the Roman Catholic Church was declared supreme on the island, with Orthodox bishops rusticated to remote hill villages.

Genoese and Venetians

During the 14th century, Cyprus shone as the easternmost Christian outpost, now that the Holy Land was permanently lost. Famagusta's merchants in particular became renowned for their extravagant wealth. The island's opulence attracted pirates, and fuelled a heated rivalry between Venetian and Genoese merchants that erupted in bloody riots in late 1372. The Cypriots sided with the Lusignans and Venetians against the Genoese, murdering merchants and looting shops in Famagusta. In retaliation, Genoa sent a fleet to ravage the island, seizing Famagusta in late 1373.

Worse followed in 1425, when the Mamelukes landed on the south coast, defeated King Janus, and rendered him a vassal of Egypt. Successor King James II was only able to oust the Genoese from Famagusta in 1464 with Egyptian funding, but it was too late to restore Lusignan power. He married a Venetian noblewoman, Caterina Cornaro, and then died (probably of Venetian poisoning); the Venetian then forced Queen Caterina to abdicate, and ruled Cyprus directly for the next 82 years.

The Venetians' lucrative trade routes were threatened by Ottoman encroachment on three sides – Anatolia, the Levant and Egypt. Imagining that attack would come from the east, the Venetians consolidated their defences mainly in Famagusta. But in mid-1570 the Turks landed on the south coast and took Nicosia after a 46-day siege. The capital's Venetian commander was killed and his head sent as a warning to Marcantonio Bragadino, commander at Famagusta. Undeterred, Bragadino led a heroic defence, with 8,000 Greek Cypriot and Italian troops holding out for over 10 months against a Turkish army of 200,000. On 1 August 1571, his ammunition gone, Bragadino surrendered. He was promised safe passage, but when Ottoman

To defend their trade, the Venetians fortified Famagusta

commander Lala Mustapha Pasha saw he had lost 50,000 men to such a tiny army, he flayed Bragadino alive. Cyprus was now a province of the Ottoman Empire.

Ottoman Rule

With the Turks controlling the whole of the eastern Mediterranean, Cyprus lost its strategic importance and was left to stagnate; local administrators usually proved more idle than oppressive. Venetians converted to Islam, and soldiers and their families, plus civilian settlers from Anatolia, were the forerunners of today's Turkish-Cypriot community. Most Greek Cypriots, who had loathed the Venetians, initially welcomed Ottoman rule, especially when the Orthodox Church was restored to supremacy. By 1660, the Sultan officially recognised the Greek Orthodox archbishop as the head of the Greek Cypriot community – and made him and his clergy responsible for collecting onerous taxes.

Pafos Fort, used by the Turkish and the British

At the start of the Greek War of Independence of 1821, the local Ottoman governor executed charismatic Archbishop Kyprianos, his three bishops and hundreds of prominent civilians, which provoked 12 subsequent years of revolt, met with massacre and plunder by Syrian and Egyptian troops.

Over subsequent decades, the Sultan tried to halt widespread abuses by tax collectors, which were provoking massive emigration of both Greek and Turkish Cypriots. But local officials opposed all reforms, often intimidating governors sent by the Sultan. The disintegration of Ottoman authority in Cyprus was symptomatic of the progressive collapse of the empire.

The British Step In

With 'the sick man of Europe' on his deathbed, the era's super powers hovered around like vultures to pick at the remains. Great Britain spent the mid-19th century fending off Russian initiatives to seize Ottoman territory; finally, in 1878, in consideration of services rendered to the Ottomans in the most recent Russo-Turkish war, occupation and administration of Cyprus (though not formal sovereignty) was ceded to Britain, whose forces landed at Larnaca in July. Once Britain acquired nearby Egypt and its Suez Canal in 1882, Cyprus' importance was reinforced.

Greek Cypriots were initially happy about the transfer of power, and came to appreciate the new schools, hospitals, law courts, aqueducts and roads furnished by British colonial administration. The population rose from 186,000 in 1881 to 310,000 in 1921. But they primarily expected the British to help Cyprus achieve *enosis*, or union with Greece, as Britain had done for the Ionian Islands in 1864.

Union with Greece was, of course, opposed by the Turkish-Cypriots. They remained confident that Britain would respect its treaty with Turkey and not give in to demands for *enosis*. In 1914, Turkey sided with the Central Powers in World War I and Britain promptly annexed Cyprus, making it a British Crown Colony. Despite infrastructure improvements, little economic growth occurred, owing to a confiscatory taxation clause of the Anglo-Ottoman treaty, in force until 1927. In 1931, Greek Cypriot members of the Legislative Council resigned, and riots broke out in Nicosia. The British response was harsh: reparations for damages, declaration of martial law, the banning of political parties and display of the Greek flag, deportation of troublemakers. But during World War II, given the British alliance with Greece against Germany, Cypriots, both Greek and Turkish, furnished 28,000 troops (and hundreds of donkeys). Political parties were duly reinstated, and local elections held.

The Fight for Enosis

In 1947, the local British governor offered limited self-rule to Cyprus, as with other colonies at the time. But the Greek-Cypriot slogan of the day was '*enosis* and only *enosis*'. In 1950 a

Statue of Archbishop
Makarios in Nicosia

plebiscite of Greek Cypriots voted 96 percent in favour of union with Greece, a vote overseen by the local church's new leader, Archbishop Makarios III (see box).

In 1955, the campaign for *enosis* became violent, led by Colonel (later General) Georgios Grivas, a Cypriot-born Greek Army officer. Directed from a hideout deep in the Troödos Mountains, EOKA (the Greek initials for the National Organisation of Cypriot Fighters) bombed public buildings and assassi-nated opponents of *enosis*. Archbishop Makarios publicly dis-owned the actions, but gave EOKA clandestine support. He was exiled in 1956, first to the Seychelles and then to Athens. In Greece itself both the government and the public gave noisy support to the Greek-Cypriot cause, which only irritated Turkey.

Turkey opposed *enosis* with two main arguments: the Turkish-Cypriot community would be defenceless if it was swallowed up in the greater Greek nation; and Greek territo-rial extension to Cyprus would pose a military threat to Turkey. In 1958, some Turkish Cypriots founded the organisation TMT to work, violently if necessary, for partition of the island.

In 1959, the foreign ministers of Turkey and Greece, plus, later, British figures and certain Cypriots, met in Zurich and London. As a result, all parties agreed to renounce either *eno-sis* or partition, while guaranteeing safeguards to protect the Turkish-Cypriot minority in a new independent republic. The first president of the republic would be Greek-Cypriot

Archbishop Makarios, and his vice-president would be the Turkish-Cypriot leader Fazil Küçük. On 16 August 1960, Cyprus became independent, though Britain retained two large military bases on the south coast. Grivas retreated, dissatisfied, to Athens.

Troubled Independence

Cabinet posts, parliamentary seats and civil service jobs were apportioned to Greek and Turkish Cypriots according to a 70:30 ratio, and the main towns elected separate Greek- and Turkish-Cypriot municipal governments, but the constitution proved unworkably complex. In late 1963, Makarios proposed 13 simplifying amendments which the Turkish Cypriots refused; fighting soon broke out in Nicosia. The British supervised a cease-fire and set up a 'Green Line' (see box page 25) separating the communities. United Nations forces were brought in to patrol the Green Line in March 1964, and they have stayed ever since. All Turkish Cypriots left their government posts on TMT orders, and many Turkish Cypriots from mixed villages

A Small Nation's Great Leader

In Archbishop Makarios, Cyprus was blessed with a first president of great intellect and spiritual authority. Born in 1913 to a peasant family in the Pafos hills, Mihail Christodoulous Mouskos became a monk at Kykkos Monastery. He studied in Athens, Istanbul and Boston, before returning to Cyprus in 1948 to become Bishop of Kition (Larnaka).

Made archbishop at the young age of 37, he won popular support with his dignified eloquence. But he was criticised by foreign observers for his failure to control Greek-Cypriot extremists, thus provoking alarm among Turkish Cypriots. Makarios, who died in 1977, impressed the world with his moral leadership of non-aligned nations at the height of the Cold War, and his courage during the Greek-inspired coup against him in 1974 and the subsequent Turkish invasion.

Kykkos Monastery, reputedly an EOKA base in the 1950s

sought shelter in fortified enclaves, which sprang up across the island. Turkey and Greece each supplemented their existing island garrisons with more officers sent to train local forces. Among them was General Grivas, in 1971, who took control of far-rightist EOKA-B (EOKA the Second). Continual attempts to reconcile the two island communities were sabotaged by outside parties, including the military junta in control of Greece since 1967.

On 15 July 1974, Greece's junta tried to impose *enosis* on Cyprus through a coup mounted by EOKA-B. The Presidential Palace was attacked, although Makarios escaped to Pafos and refuted reports of his demise with a radio broadcast. Although the illegitimate regime collapsed within eight days, the coup d'état gave Turkey a pretext to invade on 20 July. The Greek Cypriots, weakened by an ongoing civil war between leftists and EOKA-B, stood little chance, and by 14 August Turkish troops had occupied northern Cyprus. Makarios escaped to New York, where he rallied support in the UN to reinstate him as president. The Turkish army remained in control of 38 percent of the island, including Famagusta, northern Nicosia and Keryneia. Some 180,000 Greek Cypriots were forced to flee to the south, while about 44,000 Turkish Cypriots migrated to the north. By 2005, approximately 80,000 settlers had been sent to Northern Cyprus from Turkey.

In 1983, the so-called Turkish Republic of Northern Cyprus (recognised only by Turkey) was set up with Rauf Denktash as president. The UN condemned the move and urged the

leaders to find a way other than partition to protect minority rights on the island. Due to the diplomatic isolation of
the north, the economy there stagnated. The Greek Cypriot
economy, on the other hand, recovered quickly from the shock
of invasion, helped both by tourism and – represented by the
only 'legitimate' government on the island – international aid.

Successive rounds of UN-sponsored negotiations between
Denktash and the incumbent Greek Cypriot president, from
1981 onwards, got nowhere, largely thanks to Denktash's
obstructionism and post-Makarios President Spyros
Kyprianou's timidity. Much of the 1990s were spent in arms
build-ups on both sides, border incidents and mutual threats.

The oppressive rule of Denktash and his UBP party, coupled with a Turkish economic crash which dragged the North
down with it, caused the first serious Turkish-Cypriot opposi-
tion to the status quo during 2000–1, with demonstrations
and renewed intercommunal initiatives. Denktash, under continued domestic pressure, abruptly opened the Ledra Palace

The Green Line

The Green Line owes its name to the British army officer who drew a
line in green crayon on a map to separate the warring Greek and Turkish Cypriot communities in Nicosia. Since 1974, the cease-fire line has
extended across the entire island; outside the city it is generally known as
the Attila Line, after the Turks' own code designation for their invasion.
Either side of the line is a 'dead zone' (buffer zone), usually heavily mined,
varying in width from a few metres in central Nicosia to a kilometre or
so in sensitive areas. The line can now be crossed in either direction at
one of seven authorised points, by native Greek or Turkish Cypriots, and
all EU nationals. This is a marked contrast to the conditions that prevailed
before April 2003, when only non-Cypriot visitors could transit from the
South to the North on foot, with return stipulated by nightfall.

crossing of the Green Line in April 2003, allowing native Cypriots on both sides almost unconditional access to the other. Since then six other automobile or pedestrian crossings – including the highly symbolic Ledra Street/Lokmacı one in central Nicosia – have opened.

Cyprus in the EU

In tandem with Cyprus' pending EU membership on 1 May 2004, the UN presented yet another federal settlement proposal: the (Kofi) Annan Plan. Upon approval via referendum, the entire island would join the EU. The plan – conceding a huge role to Turkey – was approved 2:1 by Turkish Cypriots, but rejected 3:1 by Greek Cypriots. Nearly a decade later, the UN's patience has worn thin, with a warning that the plan can only be minimally modified.

Lately, the importance of a settlement has receded for Greek Cypriots preoccupied with the economic crisis in the South. The two largest banks were effectively bankrupt and tourism proceeds were sharply down. The winner of the 2013 presidential elections, DISY (centre-right) party chief Nicos Anastasiades, had to apply for a €16 billion EU bailout to keep Cyprus going. The same German-led 'troïka' overseeing the Greek rescue dictated harsh terms: closure of the second-largest bank, Laïki, and draconian levies on all southern bank accounts designed to raise €5.8 billion, not exempting accounts under €100,000 normally guaranteed under European banking practice. Uproar ensued as the Cypriot parliament rejected the deal; finally, on 25 March 2013, a package expropriating almost 40 percent of deposits over the guarantee limit was agreed, ending Cyprus' long-running offshore banking enterprise. The only hope of repaying the complementary €10 billion troïka loan lies in undersea natural gas fields which Cyprus is preparing to exploit with Israel, but these will not begin producing until 2017. The South faces years of economic stagnation and reduced living standards.

Historical Landmarks

c.10,000 BC First evidence of human occupation.

c.8000 BC First permanent settlements on Cyprus.

c.3500 BC Copper mines in Troödos foothills establish early wealth.

1200 BC Mycenaean Greeks settle on the island.

333 BC Alexander the Great expels Persians.

294 BC Cyprus subject to Hellenistic Egypt under the Ptolemy dynasty.

58 BC Romans annexe Cyprus to their empire.

4th century AD Christianity takes hold; many churches built.

649–53 Arabs invade and settle on the island.

963–1184 Middle Byzantine period. Cyprus flourishes.

1191–92 England's Richard the Lionheart defeats Isaac Komnenos and sells Cyprus to Guy de Lusignan, who founds a 300-year dynasty.

1489 Venetians depose the last Lusignan ruler, Caterina Cornaro.

1571 Fall of Famagusta to the Turks ends Venetian rule.

1571–1878 Period of Ottoman rule.

1878 Cyprus occupied by Britain, with Ottoman agreement.

1914 Ottomans side with Central Powers in World War I; Britain formally annexes Cyprus.

1955 EOKA begins campaign of violence in pursuit of enosis.

1959–60 Independence negotiated and granted.

1963–64 Intercommunal strife endangers young republic; UN intervenes.

1974 Coup by Greek military junta gives Turkey pretext to invade, occupying 38 percent of island.

1980s The South develops mass tourism.

1983 The 'Turkish Republic of Northern Cyprus' is declared by the North, but recognised only by Turkey.

2003 De facto border between South and North opened to free transit.

2004 The Republic of Cyprus joins the EU without Northern Cyprus.

2008 The euro is introduced in the South.

2013 Economic crisis overtakes the South; EU 'aid' package sees €5.8 billion confiscated from high-value bank accounts.

WHERE TO GO

I f you really want to get to know Cyprus, rather than just soak up sun on its beaches, you should stay in more than one place. If your base is at one of southern Cyprus' extremities – Pafos or Agia Napa – it's a good idea to spend a few nights at a more central coastal loca-tion around Limassol, or to go inland to Nicosia or the Troödos Mountains. You may also want to set aside time for the North, where the best overnight options are around Keryneia or on the Karpaz Peninsula.

NICOSIA AND ENVIRONS

Nicosia (*Lefkosia* in Greek, *Lefkoşa* in Turkish) ❶ is Cyprus' only interior city, occupying the site of ancient Ledra, founded in the 3rd century BC by Lefkonas, son of Ptolemy I of Egypt. When coastal Paphos and Salamis (Constantia) came under Arab attack during the 7th century AD, the population moved inland and Nicosia became the chief city. Under the Lusignans, it grew into a splendid capital marked by elegant churches and monasteries in the French Gothic style.

Almost everything of interest to tourists lies within, or just outside, the old city walls. The ramparts, built by the Venetians in preparation for the Turkish invasion of 1570, remain Nicosia's dominant feature. The wheel-shaped Renaissance fortification has become the modern capital's distinctive logo, with its 11

Clear waters at Petra tou Romiou on the southwest coast

Sturdy Famagusta Gate

pointed bastions and three gateways named after the coastal cities to which they lead – Famagusta Gate to the east, Pafos Gate to the west and Keryneia (Girne) Gate to the north. Some of the bastions now shelter municipal offices, while sections of the (now dry) moat serve as public gardens and car parks.

Since the Turkish invasion of 1974, Nicosia remains a divided city, roughly half in Southern Cyprus, half in the North; the buffer zone that straddles the dividing line, with its derelict 1930s buildings, UN, Greek-Cypriot and Turkish-Cypriot checkpoints, barbed wire, sandbags and roadblocks, is an eerie reminder of this. However, the Cypriot capital is experiencing something of a rebirth. Both tourists and Cypriots can now pass with relative ease between the two halves at the three local official crossing-points.

Many visitors spend just a day here, but an overnight stay (or more) is well worthwhile if you want to explore both halves of the fortified city properly – and experience some of the best dining opportunities on the island. Be prepared for real summer heat – Nicosia is around three or four degrees hotter than the coast, with temperatures soaring to 37°C (99°F) in July.

The Cyprus Museum

The island's finest collection of antiquities is housed in the **Cyprus Museum** Ⓐ (Tue–Fri 8am–4pm, Wed until 5pm, Sat 9am–4pm, Sun 10am–1pm) on Leoforos (Avenue) Mouseiou, just west of the walled city near the Pafos Gate. The neoclassical building houses archaeological artefacts dating from the Stone Age (around 8000 BC) to the Roman era, though the most riveting displays are of Bronze Age and Archaic vintage. Ground will eventually be broken across the road for a purpose-built annexe, linked to the existing building by an underpass or aerial bridge; the guards may proudly tell you that items in storage could fill four museums of comparable quality.

Exhibits from the early Bronze Age, in Room 2, include the so-called sanctuary model (2000 BC), in which worshippers and priests attend a bull sacrifice while a peeping Tom on the sanctuary wall watches the secret ceremony. In Room 3, an intriguing Mycenaean *krater* (drinking cup) imported to Enkomi in the 14th century BC has an octopus motif framing a scene of Zeus preparing warriors for battle at Troy; nearby, a beautiful green faïence *rhyton* (ritual drinking vessel) of the 12th century BC depicts a lively bull-hunt in Kition.

Highlight of Room 5 is a trio of magnificent lions, tongues and teeth bared, plus two sphinxes, discovered in 1997 guarding tombs at Tamassos. Left of these is a double-sided limestone stele depicting Dionysos on one side, and on the other, facing the wall, an erotic scene leaving nothing to the imagination.

Cyprus' Terracotta Army

Perhaps the most memorable exhibit in the Cyprus Museum is the 'Terracotta Army', consisting of over 500 votive statues and figurines dating from between 625 and 500 BC (an equal number were taken to Stockholm by the Swedish excavators). Found at Agia Irini in northwest Cyprus, the figurines are displayed as they originally stood, around the altar of an open-air sanctuary dedicated to a dual cult of war and fertility. Soldiers, war chariots, priests with bull masks, sphinxes, minotaurs and bulls were fashioned in all sizes, from life-size to just 10cm (4ins) tall, and at various levels of workmanship, according to the wealth of the donor.

At the far end of the hall, a sensuous marble Aphrodite has become the logo of island tourism despite having lost her arms and lower legs.

The monumental bronze of Roman Emperor Septimius Severus (*c.*ad 200) dominates Room 6. Highlights of Room 7 include the 'Horned God' from Enkomi, one hand downturned in a blessing gesture, and gold pieces from the Lambousa Treasure Hoard. Up short stairs in Room 11 is some fascinating royal tomb furniture from Salamis (8th century BC): an ivory throne, a bed, ornamentation for two funerary chariots and their horses' tackle.

Statue of Aphrodite

Along Odos Lidras

The old city's principal thoroughfare and main pedestrianised shopping street, **Lidras** (Ledra Street), runs north from Plateia Eleftherias to the Ledra/Lokmacı crossing. Just off its southern end, at Ippokratous 17, stands the award-winning **Leventis Municipal Museum of Nicosia** ❸ (Tue–Sun 10am–4.30pm; free but donation appreciated), three floors of a fine 19th-century neoclassical mansion devoted to the city's history as reflected in privately donated archaeological collections, Lusignan pottery, metal utensils, old engravings and posters, displays on trades or crafts, and worthwhile temporary exhibitions.

Just east of the museum spreads the so-called **Laïki Geitonia** (Popular Neighbourhood), which purports to recreate old Nicosia through various buildings in traditional style, some restored, others purpose-built, house galleries, cafés and tavernas, the latter eminently avoidable. A tourist trap, in short; the real rescue of the long-neglected old town is taking place on other streets, through private, state and UN initiatives.

Slightly further up Lidras, the **Ledra Museum-Observatory** (daily summer 10am–7pm, closes earlier Sept–May) on the top floor of the Debenhams department store, gives excellent views of the whole city, though the 'museum' bit is rather bogus, consisting merely of poor reproductions of archival photos.

East of, and parallel to, Lidras is pedestrianised Onasagorou, less chain-store dominated and with interesting restaurants or cafés. It leads north to the landmark church of **Panagia Faneromeni** (open irregularly; free), dating from 1873 in its present form and last resting place of the four bishops executed in 1821. Nearby is the chunky but handsome **Araplar Mosque,** usually closed to the public and actually the converted 16th-century church of Stavros tou Missirikou.

The Archbishop's Palace and Around

Linchpin of eastern Greek Cypriot old Nicosia is the **Archbishop's Palace** on Plateia Archiepiskopou Kyprianou, a grandiose pastiche built during the 1980s to replace its predecessor, destroyed by EOKA-B during its July 1974 putsch. The

Plateia Eleftherias

Most visitors to the old city enter via Plateia Eleftherias, a prominent square just southwest of the walled city that has been in the throes of a Zaha Hadid-designed makeover since 2008. It's currently a rather large hole in the ground, as funds to pay for the special concrete stipulated by Ms Hadid are lacking; you can see what the finished project will look like at www.zaha-hadid.com/master plans/eleftheria-square.

An icon of Christ on display at the Byzantine Museum

only portions of it generally open to the public, at the rear right as you face it, are the **Byzantine Museum and Art Galleries** ⓒ (Mon–Fri 9am–4.30pm, Sat except Aug 9am–1pm). The upper storey with its second-rate collection of religious paintings is distinctly optional, but the ground-floor galleries are essential viewing. Assembled there are superb icons rescued from all over Cyprus, but the main stars are towards the rear. Don't miss the display of seven splendid 6th-century mosaics from Panagia Kanakaria church in Northern Cyprus, recovered through court action during the 1980s and 1990s, after having been looted and offered for sale on the international art market. Immediately adjacent are the best 15th-century frescoes from Antiphonitis Monastery in the North, recovered in 1997 after having been similarly looted and illegally exported. In another corner, new to the gallery since early 2012, is more repatriated art: magnificent 13th-century frescoes from the chapel of Agios Evfimianos at Lysi in the North, comprising a Christ Pandokrator in a dome, and a Virgin flanked by angels in an apse, remounted exactly as they were in their original setting.

Next to this museum is **Agios Ioannis** (Mon–Fri 8am–noon and 2–4pm, Sat 8am–noon; free), Nicosia's small Orthodox cathedral, built in 1665 in an approximation of Late Gothic style. Its colourful 18th-century frescoes depict key moments in the island's early Christian history. The adjacent Gothic-arcaded building, all that remains of a Lusignan Benedictine monastery, is now the **Ethnographic Museum of Cyprus** (Tue–Fri 9.30am–4pm, Sat 9am–1pm), full of wooden water wheels, looms, pottery, carved and painted bridal chests, lace, embroidered costumes and much else besides.

Next door the **National Struggle Museum** (Mon–Fri 8am–2pm, also Wed 3–5.30pm except July and Aug; free), minimally labelled in English – it's meant mostly for Greek Cypriot schoolchildren – glorifies EOKA's campaign of shootings, sabotage and demonstrations, as well as documenting the harsh British reprisals. Displays include cartoons, witty graffiti, newspaper clippings, final letters of condemned prisoners and EOKA fighters' belongings.

Immediately west of the Ethnographic Museum along Palias Ilektrikis stands the **Nicosia Municipal Arts Centre D** (Sept–Jul Wed–Sat 10am–3pm and 5–11pm, Sun 10am–4pm; free) the city's primary modern-art museum, universally known as the Palia Ilektriki ('Old Electric') from its being a converted power plant. Constantly changing exhibits are generally compelling, plus there's a popular restaurant on the premises.

To experience a more successful rejuvenation project than Laïki Geitonia, it's worth strolling from the vicinity of the Archbishop's Palace towards the far northeasterly corner of the Greek-Cypriot old town, where the contiguous neighbourhoods of **Tahtakale** (with a fine old mosque) and **Chrysaliniotissa** (Khrysaliniotissa) have had their Ottoman-era mansions and humbler houses repaired and painted in a varied palette, and their interiors renovated to serve as housing for families. Heart of the latter district is the originally Lusignan church of **Panagia Chrysaliniotissa E** (Our Lady of the Golden Flax); it is rarely open, but the finely carved exterior is the main attraction, with most of its interior art

Ömeriye Mosque's minaret

now safely in the Byzantine Museum.

Immediately southeast of Tahtakale and Chrysaliniotissa is the massive tunnel-like **Famagusta Gate ⑤** (Mon–Fri May–Sept 10am–1pm and 5–8pm, Oct–Apr 10am–1pm and 4–7pm; free), originally the main entrance to the medieval city. Restored during the early 1980s as the first of the local gentrification projects, it now operates as a cultural centre. The masoned barrel vaults provide an atmospheric setting for concerts, plays and art exhibitions; check what's currently on at www.cyprus.com/pyli-ammochostou-famagusta-gate-html.

Two blocks south of the Archbishop's Palace, at Patriarchou Grigoriou 20, the **House of Hadjigeorgakis Kornesios ⑥** (Tue–Fri 8.30am–3.30pm, Wed until 5pm, Sat 9.30am–3.30pm) is a beautiful 1793 structure with a Gothic-style doorway and overhanging, enclosed balcony. The Ottoman-style interior, thoroughly renovated in 2009–11, is notable for its period furnishings, ornate stairway and grand reception room. It attests the wealth of Kornesios, the *dragoman* or official mediator between the Turkish sultan and Cypriot archbishop.

A short walk west along Patriarchou Grigoriou brings you to Plateia Tillyrias, dominated by the **Ömeriye Mosque ⑪**, transformed from the Augustinian monastic church of St Mary's by the Ottoman conquerors. The mosque is still used for Muslim worship but is open to visitors outside of prayer times. The late 16th-century **hamam** or Turkish bath across the square was meticulously restored in 2004, and functioned as a contemporary spa for many years until a legal dispute broke out concerning the municipality's re-tendering of the concession; this should be resolved by the time you read this (check progress on www.hamambaths.com), and a full range of treatments be available daily, all day.

Northern Nicosia

Compared with the bustling southern half of the city, northern Nicosia is quieter and poorer, though this is changing fast. The Lidra/Lokmacı pedestrian crossing point is conveniently close to a cluster of the most interesting sights in the North, making even the shortest visit worthwhile.

From much of the city, you will glimpse the minarets of the **Selimiye Camii** ❶ (Selimiye Mosque or Aya Sofya; daily dawn–dusk; donation expected), which was formerly the

Inside the House of Hadjigeorgakis Kornesios

Selimiye Mosque

Gothic Cathedral of the Holy Wisdom, begun in 1209 and consecrated in 1326 (though never actually completed). Here, Lusignan rulers were crowned kings of Cyprus; the Ottomans turned it into a mosque after the 1570 conquest, whitewashing over all the figural imagery but leaving soaring arches intact.

Next door, the **Bedesten** ❿ began life as a 6th-century Byzantine church before being enlarged as the Catholic church of St Nicholas of the English during the 14th century. Under the Ottomans it served briefly as a grain store and lockable cloth market before being abandoned. It emerged in 2011 from UN-sponsored renovation, so you can once again admire the building's glory – the magnificent north portal with its relief carving. Across the street is a functioning bazaar, the **Belediye Pazari** (Municipal Market), widely known as the Bandabulya. It was rebuilt in 2010–12 for structural reasons, at the cost of its former atmosphere – and the expulsion of most of the old stallholders. Across Selimiye Meydanı, beyond the apse of the Selimiye Camii, stands the **Lapidary Museum** ⓚ (Mon–Fri summer 9am–2pm, winter 9am–12.30pm and 1.30–4.30pm), a Lusignan building filled with intricately carved stonework of every description.

West of the mosque, Asma Altı Sokağı leads past a couple of old Turkish *hans* (courtyarded inns). The **Büyük Han** ⓛ

(Great Inn) – now home to small art galleries, workshops, and a café-restaurant – one of the oldest (1572) purpose-built Ottoman structures on the island, was thoroughly and tastefully restored in 1992–2002. The same cannot be said for the nearby **Kumarcılar Hanı** (Gamblers' Inn), whose restoration has been botched following its sale to a private businessman. Also nearby is the **Büyük Hamam** (Great Bath), a converted Lusignan church, which, like its South Nicosia counterpart, has been overhauled though opening hours are still erratic. At the far end of Asma Altı Sokağı is **Atatürk Meydanı** ⓜ, the hub of Turkish-Cypriot Nicosia. Its central granite column was probably brought from Salamis by the Venetians.

From the square, head north along Girne Caddesi to the **Mevlevî Tekke** ⓝ (daily summer 9am–2pm, winter 9am–1pm and 2–4.45pm). This was once a ceremonial hall used by the Mevlevî 'whirling dervish' sect, outlawed in Turkey in 1925 but surviving in Cyprus until 1954. The multi-domed, 17th-century building now has displays on the dervishes' daily life, including mannequins holding the musical instruments essential to the whirl-ing ceremony. The building itself is the star exhibit, but an arresting sight is the room packed with the tombs of 16 Mevlevî sheiks. Near here, the **Keryneia Gate** (Girne Kapısı) is northern Nicosia's only original Venetian gate, but isolated since 1931 when the British cut great gaps in the walls to either side to per-mit passage of traffic to the rest of Northern Cyprus.

Venetian coat of arms on Atatürk Meydanı

At work in the fields around Tamassos

Around South Nicosia

The following excursions all lie within 50km (30 miles) of southern Nicosia, making them easy day trips.

Tamassos (daily Apr–Oct 9.30am–5pm, Nov–March 8.30am–4pm) ❷, an ancient city-kingdom dependent on copper mining, is just over 20km (12 miles) southwest of the capital, near the village of Politiko. Here excavations have uncovered a sanctuary and altar dedicated to Aphrodite/Astarte; although its importance is difficult to appreciate given its currently ruinous state, the discovery of copper traces in the temple demonstrated that metallurgy was sacred and that priests may have controlled the enterprise. Of more general interest are two royal tombs (6th century BC). In each, stairways descend to a narrow *dromos* – a passage carved in stone to imitate wooden surfaces, complete with simulated bolted doors, window sills and 'log-roof' ceilings. A set of magnificent stone lions and sphinxes which guarded the tombs are on display at the Cyprus Museum (see page 30).

From here a scenic, back-road drive leads to the monastery of **Machairas (Makherás)** ❸, 884 metres (2,900ft) up in the rugged Pitsilia region (church open daily for pilgrims 8am–6pm; free; no cameras or videos). The monastery itself is a modern construction; an 1892 fire destroyed the original 12th-century foundation, although an allegedly miracle-working icon of the Virgin survived, and modern frescoes are of a high standard.

The region (and the monastery itself) was a hideout for EOKA's second-in-command Grigoris Afxentiou, who was burnt alive at the conclusion of a protracted battle with the British near the monastery in 1957. The site of his death (a cave just below the monastery) is decorated with wreaths and is a place of pilgrimage for Greek Cypriots; inside the monastery a one-room museum documents the man and his grisly end.

Down the road beyond Lazanias and Gourri, the officially protected but rather lifeless village of **Fikardou (Fikárdhou)** represents a worthy effort to sustain Cypriot rural traditions, rating as a Unesco World Heritage Site. Its subtly coloured 18th- and 19th-century stone and mud-straw houses along cobbled streets have been restored with intent to revitalise the community. Alas, it does not seem to be working; in 1992, when the scheme was in its infancy, there were just eight permanent residents, and the population has remained at about the same number. Wend your way past the church to the museum-houses of

Mosaic above a door at Machairas Monastery

Asinou Church's plain exterior belies the dazzling art within

Katsinioros and **Achilleas Dimitri** (June–Aug Tue–Fri 9.30am–4.30pm, Sat 9.30am–4pm, Sun 10am–1.30pm, Sept–May Tue–Fri 9am–4pm, Sat 9am–3.30pm, Sun 10.30am–2pm), where you can see authentic old furnishings, a spinning wheel and loom, an olive press and a *zivanía* still.

Asinou Church

Stranded somewhat in the middle of nowhere just outside Nikitari, 50km (31 miles) west of Nicosia, is **Panagia Asinou ❹**, also known as Panagia Forviotissa (Our Lady of the Meadows; Mon–Sat 9.30am–1pm and 2–4pm, Sun 10am–4pm; may open later in summer; free but donation appreciated), one of the gems of the Troödos foothills. From Nicosia take the road beyond Peristerona, then follow the signs to the 12th-century hillside church, famous for its magnificent Byzantine frescoes (also see page 65).

This modest but exquisite little stone-built, pitch-roofed church contains a veritable gallery of Byzantine art from the 12th century, some skilfully overpainted 250 years later. A booklet explaining the different styles and subjects of the frescoes is usually available. Failing that, the highlights are a complete cycle of the life of Christ in the middle recess of the ceiling, and the apsidal frescoes of the Virgin flanked by archangels and Christ offering Communion to the apostles. If you find the church closed go back to the village of Nikitari and search out the local priest who looks after the key – either in the central café, or by phoning tel: 99830329.

LARNAKA AND THE EAST

Sprawling along the western shore of the wide bay that bears its name, **Larnaka (Larnaca) ❺** retains a holiday resort atmosphere while at the same time hosting Cyprus' main international airport and the country's second busiest port (after Limassol).

Much of northern Larnaka is built over the ancient city-kingdom of Kition. Legend attributes its founding to the Phoenician Kittim, a grandson of Noah, but Mycenaean dwellings discovered from the 2nd millennium BC make this the oldest continuously inhabited city in Cyprus. The Phoenicians prospered here from the export of copper, and many centuries later Lusignan barons revived the town as a commercial and shipping centre. Under the Ottomans, foreign merchants and the consulates needed to protect their interests gave the town a cosmopolitan air.

Larnaka's Agios Lazaros

The Seafront

The palm-lined **Foinikoudes** (Finikoúdhes, 'Palm Trees') **Promenade** is home to hotels, chic cafés and fast-food eateries; at the north end is the pleasure-boat marina. A bust of the Athenian commander Kimon, who led a fleet to recapture Kition from the Persians in 450 BC (but died in the attempt), is a reminder of an ancient past.

From the marina, the compacted, dark-sand town beach stretches almost to the old fort that marks the edge of what was the Muslim quarter. **Larnaka Fort** (Mon–Fri June–Aug 9am–7.30pm, Sept–May 9am–5pm), originally Lusignan but adapted by the Ottomans, houses exhibits from its own history and serves as a venue for cultural events. From the ramparts, there are good views of the coastline. Opposite is the **Cami Kebir** (Great Mosque; dawn–dusk; donation expected), a converted Lusignan church still functioning as a place of worship for local Egyptians, Syrians and Iranians. Notice the tombstones topped with stone turbans in the graveyard, a rare sight so close to a mosque.

Turbanned tombstones in the Cami Kebir's graveyard

Agios Lazaros

Some 300 metres/yds inland from here looms the three-tiered campanile of the town's most revered church, **Agios Lazaros** (daily Apr–Aug 8am–12.30pm and 2.30–6.30pm, Sept–Mar 8am–12.30pm and 2.30–5.45pm; free but donation appreciated), dedicated to the man the New Testament tells us Jesus raised from the dead. According to legend, the locals of Bethany, his home town, were decidedly unimpressed by the miracle, expelling Lazarus in a not particularly seaworthy boat that nevertheless got him as far as Kition. Here, where he was more appreciated, Lazarus settled, became bishop and some 30 years later died (this time for good). The church erected over his tomb has been rebuilt many times, most recently in an extravagant mix of Byzantine, Romanesque and Gothic styles, and it has a fine iconostasis. The purported remains of Lazarus were taken from here to Constantinople in 898; in the crypt below the iconostasis you can see the empty but still venerated sarcophagus.

Larnaka's Museums

Opposite the marina, housed in refurbished former customs warehouses, are the **Larnaka Municipal Cultural Centre** (Mon–Fri 9am–1pm and 4–7pm, Sat 9am–1pm, closed Sun June–Aug; free), whose art gallery has a changing programme of exhibits by local and foreign artists. Across from the nearby tourist office, on Zinonos Kitieos, is the town's best private collection, the **Pierides Marfin Laïki Bank Museum** (Mon–Thur 9am–4pm, Fri–Sat 9am–1pm). Housed in an old family mansion are hundreds of archaeological finds and works of art from all over the island, tracing Cypriot culture from Chalkolithic to Lusignan times. Highlights include the famous 'Howling Man' of 3000 BC from Souskiou, painted Archaic and Attic pottery, cruciform picrolite idols, an antiquarian map gallery, Byzantine and Lusignan glazed ceramics, Roman glassware and Cypriot embroidery.

  Larnaka District Archaeological Museum (Tue–Fri 8am–3pm, Wed until 5pm, Sat 9am–3pm) is a 10-minute walk northwest of the city centre beyond Leoforos (Avenue) Grigori Afxentiou, on Kimonos opposite the handsome Catholic convent of St Joseph. Of principal interest here are a reconstructed tomb from nearby Choirokoitia (see page 49), and Bronze Age pottery, in particular an amphora with a rampant octopus, and a *krater* (wine goblet) in the form of a fish.

West of Larnaka

Hala Sultan Tekke, the island's most important Muslim shrine

About 3km (2 miles) south-west of the town, in the direction of the airport, lies the **Salt Lake** that provided a valuable source of income to ancient Larnaka. Lying 3 metres (10ft) below sea level, it is a true lake only in winter and early spring. The salt was once collected annually at the end of July, after the lake dried up, but today pollution has rendered it unfit for human consumption. From November to February migratory flamingos gather here, although their numbers are declining.

The **Hala Sultan Tekke** ❻ (daily June–Aug 8am–7.30pm, Apr–May and Sept–Oct 8am–6pm, Nov–Mar 8am–5pm; free but donation appreciated), seems mirage-like in summer, thrusting its minaret through greenery and palm trees beyond the blinding salt flats. This shrine contains the remains of the Prophet Mohammed's wet nurse, Umm Haram ('Sacred Mother'), known as Hala Sultan in Turkish, and is Cyprus' most important place of Muslim pilgrimage. According to tradition, Umm Haram came to Cyprus with Arab invaders in 649. She fell from her mule near the Salt Lake, broke her neck and was buried here. The present-day mosque around the tomb dates from 1816.

The outer room has brightly painted octagonal columns and a women's gallery to the right. In the inner sanctuary, the guardian (who also acts as a guide) will point out the trilithon structure above Umm Haram's grave: two enormous stones about 4.5 metres (15ft) high, covered with a meteorite said to have come from Mt Sinai and to have hovered in the air here by itself for centuries.

Some 8km (5 miles) further is the village of Kiti and its church of **Panagia Angeloktisti** ❼ (Our Lady 'Built by Angels'; daily June–Aug 8am–noon and 2–5.30pm, Sept–May 8am–noon and 2–4pm; free; photography allowed without flash). Constructed in honey-toned stone, the domed 11th-century edifice replaces a much earlier structure. Its outstanding feature is a splendid 5th- or 6th-century Byzantine **mosaic** in the apse, among the finest works of Byzantine art in Cyprus. A standing Virgin holds the Christ Child, flanked by the archangels Michael and Gabriel.

Stavrovouni, Lefkara and Choirokoitia

The famous mountain-top monastery of **Stavrovouni** ❽ (Mountain of the Cross; daily Apr–Aug 8am–noon and 3–6pm, Sept–Mar 7–11am and 2–5pm; free but donation appreciated; men only) is located just off the A1 Limassol–Nicosia motorway. At an altitude of 689 metres (2,260ft), it has superb views north to Nicosia and the hazy Pentadaktylos Mountains, and south to the Salt Lake, Larnaka and the sea.

Stavrovouni was built on the site of a shrine to Aphrodite, which, like the monastery today, was off-limits to women. Nevertheless, Helena, mother of Emperor Constantine, is said to have ventured up here in AD 327 to found the monastery and endow

Red villages

The southeast corner of Cyprus is not only a major resort area, but the island's vegetable garden. Potatoes, aubergines, tomatoes, cucumbers and onions are all grown for export in the fertile red soil of the Kokkinochoria (Red Villages) district.

it with a piece of the True Cross. The relic is still proudly displayed in the monastery church. Note that cameras or videos are forbidden anywhere in the grounds. It is really not a place for casual tourism, and there is nothing extraordinary to see other than the view; the handful of monks follow the strictest regimen on the island, based on that of Mt Athos in Greece.

At the foot of the winding road up to Stavrovouni is **Agia Varvara** (Ayía Varvára) monastery (closed noon–3pm). Most of the local monks live here, as conditions up on the exposed summit are harsh, with only a half-dozen brothers resident there at any one time. Adjacent was formerly the studio of Brother Kallinikos (1920–2011), regarded (controversially in some quarters) as one of the best icon painters of his age.

The church at the mountain-top monastery of Stavrovouni

Lefkara ❾, 40km (25 miles) west of Larnaka, is actually two villages, Pano Lefkara and Kato Lefkara, nestled in the foothills of the Troödos Mountains. Lefkara is synonymous with *lefkarítika*, the traditional embroidery that has brought the village fame for more than five centuries. Widely but incorrectly termed 'lacework', *lefkarítika* is actually linen openwork, stitched with intricate geometric patterns. Furthermore, quite a lot of what's peddled here is imported and machine-produced – beware. The village is equally renowned for its silver-smithing, and hallmarked silver jewellery may be a more reliable and better-value purchase.

Some women still work in the narrow streets and courtyards of Pano (Upper) Lefkara, patiently turning out embroidered articles which you can buy from them or in one of the many shops. There are more sales outlets than strictly neces-

Lefkara is famous for intricate lefkarítika embroidery

sary, and as a result hustling, albeit of a mild kind, is common practice.

Smaller and mostly overlooked is Kato (Lower) Lefkara, an attractive village, with many of its traditional houses recently restored and window and door frames painted in bright Mediterranean blue. In a field to one side stands the 12th-century church of **Archangelos** (always open), with damaged but still intriguing frescoes.

Archaeologically inclined visitors should head south to Choirokoitia (Khirokitiá), the modern village adjacent to the **Choirokoitia Neolithic Settlement** ❿ (daily Apr–May and Sept–Oct 8am–6pm, June–Aug 8am–7.30pm, Nov–Mar 8am–5pm). Among the oldest sites in Cyprus, it dates to just after 7000 BC. The most interesting of the four areas is the main street, with its foundations of beehive-shaped houses called *tholoi*. Artefacts discovered here are on show at Nicosia's Cyprus Museum (see page 30).

On the beach at Agia Napa

East to Agia Napa

Just beyond the resort hotels northeast of Larnaka, both A3 motorway and surface roads pass through the **Dhekelia British Sovereign Base Area**. You emerge back into Greek-Cypriot territory on the east at Xylofagou. Seaward of this is **Potamos Liopetriou ⓫**, a picturesque inlet jammed with small, gaily painted fishing boats, flanked by a couple of popular seafood tavernas.

Following the Turkish occupation of Famagusta, **Agia Napa ⓬** (Ayía Nápa) was transformed from a tiny fishing village into Cyprus' major resort. Indeed, in recent years it has become one of the Mediterranean's most notorious dance-club destinations. The change is most pronounced in the square around the monastery of **Agia Napa** (Our Lady of the Forest; daily dawn–dusk; free). The only forest here, really, is furnished by two 600-year-old giant sycamore figs in the monastery grounds.

However, during the day (when the clubbers are asleep or at the beach), the town centre is often peaceful. The monastery, built around 1530, remains one of Cyprus' most handsome Venetian buildings, with an octagonal marble fountain in the Gothic cloister. It is now a conference centre for the World Council of Churches, and its church is open regularly for Sunday services.

Agia Napa's growth is largely a result of its fine **beaches** of golden sand. The most famous one, 2km (1.2 miles) west of the centre, is **Nissi**, a picture-postcard strip and cove with limpid blue waters and a tiny island within paddling distance. At nearby **Makronisos,** another popular beach, there are 19 rock tombs dating from the classical and Hellenistic periods. East of the little port stretches **Kryo Nero,** less scenic but equally sandy.

Cape Gkreko

The coast road east towards **Cape Gkreko** ⓭, the island's southeastern tip, offers spectacular rocky inlets, caves and bays providing an escape from the crowds.

Just outside Agia Napa, beside the Grecian Bay Hotel, the **Thalassines Spilies** (Sea Caves) are famous for a much-photographed sea arch and frequented by snorkellers and divers. A few kilometres further along the main road yawn the more spectacular **Spilies sta Palatia** (Palace Caves).

Further still is the **Cape Gkreko viewpoint**. You have to walk the last 500 metres/yds uphill, but it is well worth the effort. From an altitude of almost 100 metres (330ft), the clifftop view looking west is stupendous. Just to the east is Cape Gkreko itself. The point is occupied by military installations and radio transmitters, so is accordingly off-limits.

Heading north will bring you to **Konnos Bay**, one of the most picturesque sandy

Varosha boat trip

An intriguing boat trip from Agia Napa goes as far as the marine border at Famagusta to view the decaying town of Varosha. Once a major resort, it has been left to rot since 1974, when it was declared UN territory (though it is policed by the Turkish army). Now that travel to the North has been eased, you can also drive around Varosha's outskirts on the Famagusta side, but you still can't enter or take pictures.

A view of the coast near Cape Gkreko

coves in Cyprus, with a water-sports franchise. On a quiet day, it can be heaven, though always very shallow. In midsummer, Agia Napa 'booze cruises' (or 'orgy boats') and their sound systems disturb the peace.

The coast road continues north to the purpose-built resort of **Protaras**, dominating more tiny coves like Fig Tree Bay.

LIMASSOL AND THE SOUTH COAST

Limassol ⓮ (*Lemesos* in Greek) is Cyprus' good-time town, with many restaurants, enterprising central-European hookers and lively nightlife venues. Fittingly, the city hosts the island's most exuberant pre-Lenten Carnival. In addition, it boasts Cyprus' busiest harbour and was formerly the focal point of much of the wine industry. Most accommodation is away from the centre in a strip of high-rise shoreline hotels extending 16km (10 miles) east.

Crusading English king Richard the Lionheart stopped off at Limassol in 1191, deposed the tyrannical Byzantine usurper Isaac Komnenos and then proceeded to sell Cyprus – first to the Knights Templar, subsequently to the Lusignans. The crusader Knights of St John made the environs of Limassol their headquarters in 1291, after which the town flourished for some centuries.

By the early 19th century, earthquakes and medieval raids by the Mamelukes and Genoese had reduced the city to an insignificant village. British development of the wine industry breathed new life into it and, since the 1974 partition, greater Limassol's population has almost doubled to 190,000, second only to that of Nicosia.

The only surviving medieval monument is **Limassol Castle Ⓐ**, an imposing, 13th- to 14th-century stone fortification near the old port. Today it houses the **Cyprus Byzantine and Medieval Museum** (Mon–Sat 9am–5pm, Sun 10am–1pm), the island's best collection from these periods, with some well-preserved tombstones, bronze or brass tableware, and silver plates from the Lambousa Treasure showing events from the life of King David.

The building itself, with its echoing vaults, air shafts and stairways, is equally interesting and has fine views from the battlements.

Modern sculpture on display at Limassol's seafont

The area around the castle is particularly pleasant, with lush gardens and historic buildings. Immediately south and west lies the **Lanitis Carob Mill** restoration project, with a selection of restaurants and bistros, an exhibition space, plus a small free display on the carob milling industry. The narrow lanes on all sides used be the Turkish-Cypriot commercial quarter. The **Cami Kebir** (Great Mosque) **B**, a few metres east, is still in use; there's a working Turkish bath (*hamam*) nearby. Also in this interesting quarter, you will find artisans' workshops where the speciality is copper and tin ware, plus a selection of art and ceramics galleries. The municipality is engaged in a lengthy repaving project of the district, using poor-quality materials and leaving gaping ditches – take care when strolling.

From the castle, it's a 10-minute walk along part-pedestrianised Agiou Andreou to the **Municipal Folk Art Museum** (Mon–Fri 8.30am–3pm) **C**. It provides a glimpse of rural Cypriot life through wood-carving, embroidery, jewellery and weaving; however, lighting and labelling are poor, and you must buy the guide booklet to get much out of the displays.

Further east, abutting the seafront promenade, are the **Municipal Gardens**, a pleasant place to rest for a while and the venue for the annual late-summer wine festival. At the

View of Limassol's rooftops from the castle battlements

far end of the gardens, the small **Lemesos District Archaeological Museum** (Tue–Fri 8am–3pm, Thur until 5pm, Sat 9am–3pm) **D** is – as so often in Cyprus – strongest on Archaic, Geometric and Bronze Age artefacts, in particular a *rhyton* in the form of a bull and small fertility idols with upraised arms, clasping their breasts or holding sacred mirrors of Aphrodite/Astarte.

Stone carvings in Limassol's Folk Art Museum

East of Limassol

Some 13km (8 miles) east of the town, between two clusters of beach hotels, are the ruins of ancient **Amathous** (daily June–Aug 8am–7.30pm, Apr–May and Sept·Oct 8am–6pm, Nov–Mar 8am–5pm), one of the island's oldest city-kingdoms. The remains are centred on its *agora* (marketplace), and include basilicas, a temple of Aphrodite and an elaborate waterworks system.

About 16km (10 miles) further on by motorway or surface road is **Governor's Beach** (Akti Kyvernitou) **15**, actually several coves of dark sand contrasting sharply with white-chalk cliffs just behind. There are a few tavernas and clusters of low-rise accommodation right behind. Farther east along the coast, you reach **Zygi 16**, a former carob pod-loading port with a small marina and a cluster of seafood restaurants popular with Cypriots – though almost all the fare on offer is frozen or imported.

West of Limassol

Traces of one of the earliest phases of human presence on the
island – hunters of pygmy hippos from 9000 BC – were found
on the **Akrotiri Peninsula** west of Limassol. Nearly half of
the peninsula is made up of salt marsh, frequented by migratory birds, notably pink flamingos, from October to March.
On the east coast of the peninsula is hard-packed **Lady's Mile
Beach**, popular with Lemessans. Most of the peninsula is
occupied by the airfield and other installations of the British
Akrotiri Sovereign Base Area.

Just north of the peninsula, the impressive 15th-century
Kolossi Castle ⓲ (daily June–Aug 8am–7.30pm, Apr–May
and Sept–Oct 8am–6pm, Nov–Mar 8am–5pm) is one of
the icons of Cypriot tourism. Once the headquarters of the
Knights of St John, this is the base from where they adminis-
tered their considerable sugar plantations and vineyards. The
three-storey Commanderie, as the headquarters was known,
gave its name to their prized Commandaria dessert wine, still
produced today by commercial wineries.

Among the rooms, all now empty, a middle-storey one
with a huge fireplace was the kitchen; in the adjacent room
is a damaged fresco, the only surviving decoration. Climb
the steep, narrow spiral staircase for the view from the battlements. Outside you can see traces of an ancient aqueduct and
an imposing Gothic sugar refinery.

Kourion

Before exploring the great archaeological site of Kourion,
stop in nearby Episkopi village to do a little homework at
the **Kourion Archaeological Museum** (Mon–Fri 8am–
3pm, Wed until 5pm), which holds dramatic finds from the
earthquake that devastated Kourion in AD 365. On display
is a touching group of three human skeletons: archaeologists believe them to be of a 25-year-old male protecting a

19-year-old female with an 18-month-old baby clutched to her breast. Other exhibits include a Roman stone lion fountain, terracotta vases and figurines.

Just west of Episkopi is **Kourion**  itself (daily June–Aug 8am–7.30pm, Apr–May and Sept–Oct 8am–6pm, Nov Mar 8am–5pm). Along with Salamis in the north (see page 84), this is the island's most important archaeological site, spectacularly set on a bluff above Episkopi Bay. Today, there's a broad, popular beach with a few shack-like tavernas at the base of the palisade.

Experts attribute the foundation of the town to Mycenaean settlers during the 13th century BC. Known as Curium to the Romans, it converted to Christianity in the 4th century; after the Arab raids of the 7th century, the bishopric moved to Episkopi, leaving Kourion to sink into oblivion.

Your first stop should be the reconstructed **Roman theatre** (AD 50–175), spectacularly perched on the edge of the bluff.

Kourion's Roman theatre

The remains of a public bathhouse

The theatre once seated 3,500 and is now used for early-summer performances of Shakespeare plays, and concerts. Behind the theatre is the 4th-century AD **Annexe of Eustolios**. The floor mosaics of birds and fish indicate that Eustolios was a man of wealth and taste; a long inscription to Christ suggests that he was also a Christian convert. Eustolios later added an adjacent bathhouse, which he opened to destitute survivors of the earthquake, as attested by another inscription. Its central room features some more remarkable mosaics, including one of Ktisis, the female spirit of creation, wielding a Roman foot-ruler.

The extensive ruins of the city centre, 300m northwest along a graded path, include the *agora* (marketplace) with its *nymphaeum* (fountain house). Turn to the left to explore the remains of an early Christian **basilica**. The basilica's plan reveals 12 pairs of granite columns, recycled ancient masonry, for the nave. To the north is the **baptistry**, where new converts disrobed and were anointed with oil before descending to the cross-shaped font.

On the other side of the walkway is the **House of the Gladiators,** so named for its mosaics of two duels, one with an aristocratic-looking referee – perhaps the owner of the house. Nearby, also under a protective canopy, is the **Achilles mosaic.** It depicts Achilles, disguised as a woman to avoid enlistment in the expedition to Troy, being tricked by Odysseus into grabbing a spear and shield and revealing his identity.

The **Sanctuary of Apollo Hylates/Ylatis**  (daily, same hours as Kourion; separate charge) lies 3km (2 miles) to the west. Apollo was worshipped here as god of the woodlands as early as the 8th century BC, but most of the present structures were put up around AD 100 and destroyed in the earthquake of 365.

From the ticket booth, take the path west to the pilgrims' entrance (through the remains of the Pafos Gate). The buildings here were probably hostels and storehouses for worshippers' votive offerings. The surplus was carefully placed in the *vothros* pit (at the centre of the site), which was full of terracotta figurines, mostly horse riders – still intact when uncovered by the archaeologists. Follow the sanctuary's main street to the **Temple of Apollo**, which has been partially reconstructed to look as it did in AD 100.

West to Petra tou Romiou

If the flat, hard-packed sands of Kourion Beach don't appeal to you, try the looser,

House of the Gladiators, Kourion

coarse sand-and-shingle of **Avdimou** (Evdhímou) Beach, about 10km (6 miles) further west, with two tavernas. But if you crave the creature comforts of a resort, then continue on to **Pissouri** ⓴. The latter is an attractive, sheltered place, with a coarse but fairly long sand-and-shingle beach, plus ample accommodation and eating opportunities just behind.

The Sanctuary of Apollo Ylatis

West of Pissouri, just beyond the border into Pafos district, a huge sea-washed monolith juxtaposed with white cliffs behind is the famous **Petra tou Romiou** ㉑. This is named for legendary Byzantine hero Digenis Akritas, aka Romios, who used the big rock (*pétra* in Greek) plus smaller ones around it as missiles against Arab seaborne raiders. Opposite the rocks, along the B6 road, a parking area gets very crowded at sunset. The beach here is mostly coarse gravel, and the water is often storm-stirred.

TROÖDOS MOUNTAINS

The **Troödos (Troödhos) Mountains** in central Cyprus are the island's principal upland – and pronounced, approximately, 'troh-dhos' rather than 'true-dos' as many foreigners are apt to say. They provide many things: a breath of fresh air for hot and flustered visitors and locals, a splendid collection of tiny Byzantine churches scattered around the hillsides, wonderful walking trails and, most importantly, much of the island's fresh water.

Roads up the mountain climb through foothills with rushing streams and orchards, past villages perched on the slopes, surrounded at higher altitudes by pine forest. Historically, monks and Greek-Cypriot EOKA fighters found refuge here; more recently the monasteries have been joined by resort hotels, with even a little winter skiing near the resort of Troödos. On the southern slopes in Limassol district, up to the 1,000-metre (3,300ft) contour, are the vineyards and villages that produce most of Cyprus' wine.

Platres to Troödos

At an altitude of 1,128 metres (3,700ft), **Pano Platres** ㉒ makes a good base for visiting the entire Troödos region. This little 'hill station' occupies a charming and shady mountain site and comprises several hotels, large numbers of private villas, restaurants and shops. The main pastime here is walking,

Petra tou Romiou, where Aphrodite first emerged from the sea

Typical village in the Troödos Mountains

and the Cyprus Tourism Organisation has marked several nearby mountain trails, aimed at most ability levels – get details at the Platres tourist office. The most popular hike is the 2km (1.2-mile) one up to the pretty **Kaledonia Falls**. The walk starts at the Psilodendhro restaurant and trout farm just outside Platres, and is well marked.

Omodos (Ómodhos) ㉓, renovated as a showpiece wine-producing village, lies 8km (5 miles) southwest of Platres. It's an attractive place, but has become over-commercialised, and the tour buses diminish the atmosphere their occupants have come to savour. However, you can still find calm in the village's monastery of **Timios Stavros** (True Cross), which dominates the broad, cobbled square in front of it – probably an example of Lusignan urban planning.

All roads in the mountains seem to lead to the eponymous resort of **Troödos** ㉔, which at 1,676 metres (5,500ft) is the island's highest facility. There are ski slopes nearby, while in spring and autumn it's a good starting point for dedicated ramblers. Avoid midsummer, when its single main street turns into an overcrowded promenade of kitsch stalls and rumbling tour buses. Just off this 'high street', a **visitor centre** (daily 10am–4pm) helps orientate visitors to the high mountains, and provides maps and information on the local wildlife and plants.

Mt Olympos (1,952 metres/6,404ft), Cyprus' tallest peak, also known locally as Chionistra (Khionístra, 'Snow-Tipped'), is best visited by car up a narrow road. For security reasons, you have to walk the final distance up to the giant British radar 'golf ball' and Cypriot installations on the double-humped summit, and the views are surprisingly limited. It's preferable to tackle one of two nature trails – the Atalante or the Artemis – that circle the peak.

Kakopetria and Galata

Kakopetria ㉕, chief village of the Solea region north of the Troödos ridgeline, is easily reach by fast roads from Nicosia, and is accordingly popular at weekends and holidays. The highlight of the place is its ridgeline **old quarter**, a protected ensemble that's now home to recommendable eating and accommodation. This historic part of town is essentially one long, narrow street running parallel to the leafy river. Its houses with their river-view balconies have been restored to bring out the subtle russet, amber and silver hues of the local stone.

Just outside the village is one of the Troödos Mountains' most famous frescoed churches, **Agios Nikolaos tis Stegis** (St Nicholas of the Roof; Tue–Sat 9am–4pm, Sun 11am–4pm; free but donation

Goddess' birthplace

Petra tou Romiou has long inspired legends, as before Digenis Akritas' time it was reputed to be the birthplace of Aphrodite, who emerged from the sea here (though Kythera island in Greece also strenuously claims this honour).

Old Kakopetria

appreciated). The name refers to the upper roof of shingles, built in the 15th century to shelter the older domed roof of tiles. Inside, the oldest frescoes date from the church's foundation in the 11th century, but the most unusual ones – including the Virgin nursing the infant Jesus, and the Angel at the Tomb – are from some centuries later.

Just north of Kakopetria, **Galata** ㉖ has another Unesco-listed church of 1502, **Panagia tis Podithou**; the key-keeper can be contacted at the café or on 9634 8896. Although its very Italianate fresco decoration was never completed, what exists – including an extravagantly secular Crucifixion over the west door, Solomon and David flanking the Communion of the Apostles in the apse – justifies the trouble of gaining admission. The same key-keeper will then escort you to **Archangelos** (aka Panagia Theotokou) nearby, dating from 1514 and containing an unusually complete cycle portraying the life of Christ.

Marathassa

Easily reached either from Troödos resort or from Kakopetria, the **Marathassa** valley west of Solea is home to more mountain villages and painted churches. From either start point, the first village reached is **Pedoulas** ㉗, famous for its cherries

– and its church of **Archangelos Michail** (daily 10.30am–
5pm; free but donations welcome), built in 1474. Vivid
frescoes, cleaned during the 1980s, include The Sacrifice of
Abraham, and a Baptism complete with fish in the River
Jordan. In **Moutoullas** village, 3km (2 miles) downhill,
you'll find the earliest of the frescoed churches, **Panagia tou
Moutoulla**, built in about 1280 (daily 8.30am–4pm). The
frescoes, while not the most expressive hereabouts, are unre-
touched and idiosyncratic. If time is short, prioritise attractive
Kalopanagiotis (Kalopanayiótis) village ㉘, 1km (0.5 miles)

Frescoed Churches

The Troödos Mountains' remarkable painted churches were built between the 11th and the 16th centuries. For visitors, their astonishing
degree of preservation and the beauty of their artwork makes for com-
pulsive viewing. For scholars, the churches provide a fascinating lesson in
provincial Byzantine and post-Byzantine art; there is nothing else like them
in the Mediterranean other than the country churches of Crete and Rho-
des. The original function of the frescoes was as religious cartoon strips,
teaching the simple, illiterate and often isolated parishioners the lessons of
the Gospels; today they serve as a fascinating document of Lusignan and
Venetian life, as the painters – mostly anonymous – interpreted Biblical ep-
isodes with contemporary medieval personalities and dress. Most of the
churches have been listed on Unesco's World Cultural Heritage register.

The densest concentration of painted churches lies on the north
slopes Troödos, where Panagia Asinou (see page 42), Agios Nikolaos tis
Stegis (in Kakopetria), Panagia tis Podithou (in Galata), Agios Ioannis Lambadistis (in Kalopanagiotis) and Panagia tou Araka (near Lagoudera) are all
within a short drive of each other. Some have set visiting hours; in other
cases you will have to contact the key-holder, either a priest or lay person,
who lives nearby. Mobile phone numbers are usually posted on the church
door. Photography, certainly with flash or tripod, is rarely if ever allowed.

further along, whose star is the intact riverside monastery of **Agios Ioannis Lambadistis** (daily May–Oct 9am–noon and 2–5pm, Nov–Apr 9am–noon and 1–4pm; free). The main church is actually triple, with different fresco cycles completed at various times between the 13th and 15th centuries; most of them have been carefully restored since 2009 by students of London's Courtauld Institute of Art. The northernmost, Latin chapel, with the most complete Italo-Byzantine sequence on the island, was clearly painted by a local artist who had spent extensive time in Italy. In one wing of the monastery buildings is a rewarding gallery of Byzantine and post-Byzantine icons.

Frescoed dome in the church at Lagoudera

West to Kykkou

The main roads west from either Pedoulas or Kalopanagiotis lead quickly to the monastery of **Panagia tis Kykkou** ㉙ (pronounced Tchýkou in dialect: daily June–Oct 10am–6pm, Nov–May 10am–4pm; free but charge for museum), proudly remote from the world on a mountainside surrounded by pine forest.

Kykkou is the richest and most important monastery on the island. Founded in 1094 by a hermit, it grew in prestige when Emperor Alexis Komnenos (ruled 10801–1118) gave it a rich land grant and an icon of the Virgin supposedly painted by St Luke, but now covered in gilded silver. Its legendary rain-making powers still bring in farmers to pray in times of drought.

Kykkou Monastery

But apart from the precious icon and a few other pieces, there is little of historical value here, since the monastery was gutted by fire four times between 1365 and 1813. Frankly garish mosaics and frescoes lining every vertical surface are workmanlike at best. Kykkou is primarily a place of pilgrimage and a preferred venue for baptisms, when proud relatives cheerfully ignore the ban on photography and videoing enforced against the heterodox, who can occasionally be met with faint hostility. In the quieter museum you can learn about Kykkou's history and see some of its finest treasures.

Kykkou is also famous for having had Archbishop Makarios among its novices (he is buried on a hill above the monastery). During the 1950s, Kykkou served as a communications and supply base for EOKA, and thus became a symbol of the Cypriot nationalist struggle.

West of Kykkou, onward roads lead downhill into the **Cedar Valley** (Koilada tou Kedron) 30, one of the signal successes of the island's reforestation programme. This steep-sided ravine hosts thousands of indigenous cedar trees (*Cedrus brevifolia*), first cousins to the more famous cedars of Lebanon. Nearby, around Tripylos peak, is a small reserve dedicated to the protection of the indigenous, formerly endangered Cypriot wild mountain sheep, the moufflon.

Fishing boats in Pafos harbour

Eastern Troödos churches

If you've developed a taste for frescoed churches, there are several more in the eastern half of the Troödos, easily accessible from Platres or Kakopetria. The most spectacular of these, just north of **Lagoudera** (Lagoudherá) village **31**, is **Panagia tou Araka** (Our Lady of the Wild Vetch), with most frescoes dating from 1192. The more unusual include a fine dome Pandokrator (Christ in Majesty), the only one in the Troödos, and adjacent, finely observed Presentations of Christ and the Virgin near the apse.

In **Pelendri** (Peléndhri) **32**, 14th-century **Stavros** at the village outskirts (key-keeper lives adjacent) features scenes from the life of the Virgin. Much closer to Limassol, **Louvaras** village **33** can offer deceptively tiny **Agios Mamas** church, crammed full of well-preserved frescoes from 1495 by Philip Goul, one of the few identified local painters.

Off the eastern edge of the Troödos, at **Palaichori** **34**, you'll find another member of the roster of Unesco mountain

churches, **Metamorfosis tou Sotiros** (Transfiguration of the
Saviour), dating from the 15th and 16th centuries and containing (predictably) a fine representation of the Transfiguration.

PAFOS AND THE WEST

Once a sleepy fishing port, **Pafos** (Páphos) ❸ has been transformed into a booming resort town. But visitors who want
more than just sun and sand have plenty to occupy them.
Ancient Nea Paphos was Cyprus' Roman capital and has a
wealth of historic sites. It is also a good base for exploring
nearby hill-villages and the rugged Akamas Peninsula.

Legend attributes the founding of nearby Palaia (Old)
Paphos to the priest-king Kinyras, and that city-kingdom
gained renown as the centre of Aphrodite's cult. The last
king of Palaia Paphos, Nikokles, established the port of Nea
(New) Paphos during the 4th century BC, though Palaia
Paphos remained the centre of Aphrodite worship until the
4th century ad. Within 100 years of its founding, Nea Paphos
surpassed Salamis as the chief city of Cyprus. However, earthquakes in 332 and 342 and the Arab attacks of the 7th century
forced most of the population inland to Ktima. Medieval Pafos
languished as a miserable, unsanitary seaport; however, under
the British the population gradually rose from about 2,000 to
about 9,000 in 1960. It continued to grow and prosper, with
the opening of Pafos International Airport in 1985 firmly
establishing it as a resort, and later as a major second- (or first-)
home venue for foreigners.

Kato Pafos

Heavily developed Kato (Lower) Pafos, along the seaside, is
where most visitors stay. The harbour still provides a picturesque haven for fishing and excursion boats as it curves around
a jetty to the **Medieval Fort** ❹ (daily June–Aug 8am–7.30pm,

Apr–May and Sept–Oct 8am–6pm, Nov–Mar 8am–5pm), all that remains of a much larger Lusignan castle. The Ottomans used it as a prison, the British as a salt warehouse; it is currently empty, with only the rooftop views justifying the admission fee.

With the harbour on your left, walk towards the large, modern shed-like building in the distance. Beyond this lie the famous **Paphos Mosaics** B (daily June–Aug 8am–7.30pm, Apr–May and Sept–Oct 8am–6pm, Nov–Mar 8am–5pm). These splendid decorative floors were uncovered in the remains of luxurious Roman villas of the 2nd to the 5th centuries ad. The 'houses' are named after the mosaics' most prominent motifs. The **House of Dionysos** displays the god of wine riding a chariot drawn by two panthers, flanked by satyrs and slaves. This and other scenes, such as Dionysos offering a bunch of grapes to the nymph Akme, and Ikarios of Athens getting shepherds drunk with their first taste of

The Medieval Fort in Pafos

wine, were customary decorations for banqueting halls. The **House of Aion** has a spectacular five-panelled mosaic, whose central panel depicts Aion, god of eternity, judging a beauty contest between a smug-looking Queen Cassiopeia (the winner) and unhappy, prettier water nymphs departing on assorted sea-monsters. The single other villa open to

Ancient ruins in Pafos

the public, the **House of Theseus**, features the first bath of the infant Achilles.

A short walk north leads to the restored **Odeion** , a small theatre dating from the 2nd century ad, built entirely of hewn limestone blocks. In a picturesque hillside setting, it seats 1,250 spectators for musical and theatrical performances held occasionally in the summer. Excavations continue in the adjacent **agora**, by a team from the Jagiellonian University of Krakow.

Kato Pafos to Ktima

From the harbourside car parks and public bus terminal, first Apostolou Pavlou, and then Stassandrou, climb towards the remains of 4th-century AD **Agia Kyriaki** basilica . Amid the ruins of the seven-aisled church, you can make out mosaic pavements with floral and geometric patterns and columns of green-and-white marble imported from Greece. Arabic graffiti on the columns dates from the invasion that destroyed the basilica in 653. One of the columns is called **St Paul's Pillar**, to which the apostle was (apocryphally) tied and lashed 39 times for preaching the Gospel. Amid the ruins is handsome

Pafos is famed for its Roman mosaics

post-Byzantine **Panagia Chrysopolitissa** church, sometimes also referred to as Agia Kyriaki.

A little further along Apostolou Pavlou is the intriguing sight of a tree festooned with hundreds of handkerchiefs and rags. It marks the **Catacomb of Agia Solomoni**, once regarded as a spot where prayers could be miraculously answered, and still doing a good trade with believers today. The tradition of tying a handkerchief or rag as a votive offering to a tree or bush at a sacred site is common in the Middle East. Just north of here, hacked out of the living rock on Fabrica hill, is the Australian-excavated **Hellenistic theatre E**, one of the largest on Cyprus.

Still further northwest is ancient Nea Paphos' necropolis, the so-called **Tombs of the Kings F** (daily June–Aug 8am–7.30pm, Apr–May and Sept–Oct 8am–6pm, Nov–Mar 8am–5pm). The title is a misnomer, as the subterranean burial chambers hacked out of the soft rock here between the 3rd century BC and the 3rd century AD were meant for the local privileged class, not kings. The tomb architecture is based on Ptolemaic adaptations of Macedonian prototypes: spacious courtyards with Doric columns and decorative entablatures. Of the eight tomb complexes, numbers 3, 4 and 8 are the best.

Ktima

Set on a blufftop above the resort, the upper part of Pafos, known as **Ktima**, is a normal Cypriot provincial town compared to the coastal strip. After shopping at the colourful daily produce market and a variety of souvenir stalls, you can sit down for a drink or a meal in the narrow lanes of the old centre.

There are two small museums in the centre of Ktima. The **Ethnographic Museum G** (also known as the Eliades Collection; Exo Vrysis 1; Mon–Sat 10am–5.30pm, Sun 10am–1pm), occupies a charming 19th-century house. It combines priceless antiques, a mocked-up rural room, basketry, old wagons and – in the garden – a genuine, 3rd-century BC rock tomb. Nearby, in a wing of the Bishop's Palace, the **Byzantine Museum** (Mon–Fri 9am–3pm, Sat 9am–1pm) displays icons salvaged from local chapels, including the oldest known on the island, an 8th- or 9th-century icon of St Marina.

Within the Tombs of the Kings

The remoter **Pafos District Archaeological Museum H** (Tue–Fri 8am–3pm, Wed until 5pm, Sat 9am–3pm), on the road to Limassol, houses some remarkable sculptures found in the House of Theseus (see page 71), including a statue of Asklepios (the Greek master of medicine) feeding an egg to the snake coiled around his

staff. Also, look out for the Hellenistic clay hot-water bottles, specially moulded to fit all parts of the body.

Southeast of Pafos

Just southeast of Pafos is the village of **Geroskipou** (Yeroskípou) **36**, whose name derives from **Hieros Kipos**, meaning 'Sacred Garden'; pilgrims would stop here on their way to Aphrodite's temple at Palaia Paphos. The 11th-century church of **Agia Paraskevi** (Mon–Sat Apr–Oct 8am–1pm and 2–5pm, Nov–Mar 8am–1pm and 2–4pm; free) in the centre of Geroskipou is a rare island example of a six-domed basilica. Inside are fine, if damaged, 15th-century murals and a much-revered icon from the same period, with a *Virgin and Child* on one side and a *Crucifixion* on the reverse.

In a restored house nearby is a **Folk Art Museum** (daily 8.30am–4pm). Typical of a rich Cypriot's dwelling in the late 18th or early 19th century, the upper storey is ringed with handsome wooden balconies. Display rooms are thematic, devoted to crafts such as carding and ginning cotton, spinning and weaving, tinning vessels, and a reproduced cobbler's workshop.

From here, continue southeast along the B6 for about 12km (8 miles) to **Kouklia** **37**, once Palaia Paphos (Palaipaphos), where the cult of Aphrodite was celebrated. The rites of the love goddess flourished at the **Sanctuary of Aphrodite** (daily 8am–4pm, Wed 8am–5pm). Most of the valuable finds have been taken to Nicosia, though after much bureaucratic wrangling the original of the famous 2nd- or 3rd-century AD mosaic of *Leda and the Swan* has been returned. It has pride of place in the **Palaipaphos Museum** (same hours as the Sanctuary; same ticket), inside the sturdy Château de Covocle (originally a Lusignan manor-farm). The museum galleries are upstairs from a 13th-century vaulted banquet hall, the acoustically superb venue for early summer chamber music concerts. Those with their own transport may want to continue inland to the so-called **Palaia Enkleistra** (key and instructions from museum staff in exchange for piece of ID), a 15th-century cave-hermitage with damaged but unique frescoes; on the ceiling, dating from the era when the Western and Orthodox churches were briefly united, is a rare depiction of the Holy Trinity.

North of Pafos

Beaches in Pafos are unremarkable, so many visitors travel 10km (6 miles) north to better sands at **Coral Bay** (Kolpos Koralion). Further up the coast, there are more beaches either side of **Agios Georgios (Áyios Yeóryios),** which has accommodation, restaurants and the remains of a basilica with mosaic flooring (free access). Beyond pebbly 'White River

Remains of fluted columns at the sanctuary of Aphrodite

The monastery of
Agios Neofytos

Beach' just north of Agios Georgios, you'll pass sandier **Toxeftra** beach, and the turning inland to the famous **Avgas Gorge**, a favourite destination for hikers. Beyond here, it's best to have a 4WD vehicle as you head up to Cape Lara and the vast sandy beaches on either side. The northerly, duny **Lara Bay** ❸ is an official marine reserve, set aside to protect the endangered green and loggerhead turtles that come ashore on summer nights to hatch and bury their eggs.

Some 9km (5 miles) northeast of Pafos, the monastery of **Agios Neofytos** ❸ (Áyios Neóphytos; daily Apr–Oct 9am–1pm and 2–6pm, Nov–Mar 9am–1pm and 2–4pm; charge for Hermitage) dominates a wooded slope. Its church has fine 16th-century frescoes and icons, but the main focus is the 12th-century **Enkleistra** (Hermitage), around which the monastery grew. The saintly historian and theologian Neophytos (1134–1219) supposedly hacked this cave-dwelling out of the rock with his own hands and then supervised the creation of the frescoes that decorate the chapel and cell. One shows Neophytos himself, being escorted into Paradise by two archangels.

On the north coast 35km (22 miles) from Pafos, the small town of **Polis** ❹ stands where the ancient citykingdom of Marion once thrived from nearby gold and copper mines. Archaeological finds from the site are on display at the **Marion-Arsinoe Archaeological Museum** (Tue–Fri

8am–3pm, Wed until 5pm, Sat 9am–3pm). The old town centre has been restored and has a pleasant if touristy cluster of cafés and restaurants. Polis is a prelude to the fishing port and beach resort of **Lakki** (Latchí) **㊶**, where seafood tavernas cluster around the 1992-improved fishing port; to either side are decent sand-and-pebble beaches.

A Wilderness Under Threat

Untamed and scenic, the last major piece of unspoilt coastline in South Cyprus, the Akamas Peninsula arouses strong passions, among conservationists, hikers and wildlife-spotters on the one hand, and tourist-enterprise developers, the Orthodox Church and local villagers on the other. Since 1986, organisations as disparate as the World Bank, the European Union, Friends of the Earth and Greenpeace have called for the creation of a local national park. Matters are complicated by the entire peninsula being a patchwork of private land (Greek- and Turkish-Cypriot owned), state forest, village commons and Church holdings. The British Army, who long used the peninsula as a firing range, departed in 1999 after sustained environmentalist protest, but ironically their presence had a preservationist effect. Until stopped from doing so, the Church removed sand from west-coast beaches to fill traps at Tsada golf course. Hunters, out in force on Wednesdays and Sundays during winter, also agitate against any protection regime. Since the millennium, and in particular since 2005, government proposals have envisioned a reserve much reduced in size and strictness from original plans, and 'controlled' development. The major player in the latter is Carlsberg magnate Photos Photiades, whose extensive north-coast property he would like to turn into a luxury resort. Various schemes for compensation or land-swaps have been proposed to induce him (and other owners) to leave. However, with the sharp economic downturn and the equally sharp drop in tourist numbers, such a resort (or payouts) seem increasingly unlikely, and any final decision has been put on hold for now.

The rugged landscape of the Akamas Peninsula

Romantics should head west to the end of the paved road, from where it's a brief stroll to the **Baths of Aphrodite** ⓵, a small, shaded natural pool and springs set in a cool green glade, where the goddess was wont to bathe. Meatier hikes – either a coastal track giving swimming opportunities, or more challenging proper trails uphill – lead from here further into the **Akamas Peninsula**, one of the few unspoilt wildernesses left on the island and long a battleground between environmentalists and developers (see box).

Notheast along the coast from Polis, a scenic route leads through relatively undeveloped seafront villages and past secluded beaches near **Pomos** and **Pachyammos** (Pahýammos). Beyond the latter, the road snakes through the steep hills of Tillyria to avoid the Turkish military enclave of Kokkina (Erenköy), before reaching the Cypriot-patronised resort of **Kato Pyrgos** ⓵, no longer the end of the line since a crossing point to the North opened nearby in 2009.

NORTHERN CYPRUS

The Turkish-occupied north, which comprises around 38 percent of the island, contains some of Cyprus' most beautiful landscapes, best beaches, most dramatic monuments and two of its most historic towns. Partition and the subsequent political isolation long helped preserve the countryside from the ravages of mass tourism, but since 2000 development around Keryneia in particular has been every bit as intensive as anywhere in the South.

It is possible to whizz around Northern Cyprus in a day and cover – or at least glimpse – some of the main highlights, although unless you are short on time, this is not recommended. In three or four days you can see all the sights, including northern Nicosia (see page 37), at a more leisurely pace.

The Mountain Castles

North of Nicosia, the Mesaoria plain (Mesarya in Turkish) rises abruptly at the **Keryneia Hills**, which Lawrence Durrell, who lived in their shadow from 1953 to 1956, described as 'par excellence the Gothic range, for it is studded with crusader castles pitched on the dizzy spines of the mountains, commanding the roads which run over the saddles between'. The range's most striking peak is **Pentadaktylos** (Beşparmak, 'Five Fingers').

The three castles now lie in noble ruin, victims not of enemy bombardment but of partial demolition by the Venetians. Most extensive is **Agios Ilarion ⓸** (daily summer 8am–6pm, winter 9am–4.30pm), which climbs along knife-edge ridges in three tiers of battlements and towers, reaching an altitude of 670 metres (2,200ft) under twin peaks, with steps leading up and down in all directions.

The castle was built in the 10th century around an earlier church and monastery honouring the hermit Hilarion, who fled here when the Arabs took Syria. The original Byzantine

Pentadaktylos (Five Finger) Mountain

structure was fortified and extended by the Lusignans as a summer residence. The views down to Keryneia harbour are superb and, on a clear day, you can see the mountains of southern Turkey some 100km (60 miles) away.

Another dramatic, if small, ruinous castle is **Buffavento** ⑮ ('Buffeted by the Winds'; unrestricted access), just off the easterly major road over the Pentadaktylos. This is Cyprus' highest fortress, at 940 metres (2,991ft), with views over literally half the island, especially towards dusk when there's the spectacle of Nicosia turning on its lights.

Keryneia (Girne)

Offering the most beautiful sheltered harbour in Cyprus and a grand old castle, the charming town of **Keryneia** ⑯ – Girne in Turkish, still Kyrenia to most Greek Cypriots and expats – is the most strikingly situated on the island. The venerable buildings that line the port have almost all been converted into bars or restaurants of indifferent quality, but the setting is so irresistible that most every visitor patronises them at least once.

Overlooking the harbour is massive **Keryneia Castle** (daily summer 9am–7pm, winter 9am–4.15pm), whose fortifications date mostly from the Venetian era. Today, its walls enclose a Byzantine chapel, royal apartments and various historical displays, including the **Kyrenia ship**, the oldest wreck ever recovered from the seabed (and featured on three Cypriot euro coins). This Greek trading ship sank in 30 metres (100ft)

Visiting the North

There are currently seven crossing-points along the buffer zone that separates North and South. There are two crossings for pedestrians in central Nicosia: Lidras/Lokmacı in the Old City and at the former Ledra Palace Hotel close to the Pafos Gate. Border crossings for vehicles are at Agios Dometios/Metehan in the western suburbs of Nicosia; at Pyla/Pergamos (Beyarmudu), handiest for Karpasia; the so-called 'Four Mile' crossing within the Dhekelia British Sovereign Base Area, direct to Famagusta (Gazimağusa); at Astromeritis-Kato Zodeia (Boştancı), near Morfou (Güzelyurt); and Kato Pyrgos (Günebakan) on the north coast, allowing fast transit from the Polis area towards Nicosia.

The procedure for crossing is straightforward, though at weekends, and at Agios Dometios/Metehan especially, there can be long queues. Officially the border opens at 8am and closes for returning visitors at midnight, but the Nicosia crossings in particular tend to be open almost around the clock. The Greek Cypriot police will view, but not stamp, your passport going in each direction; the Turkish Cypriot police will, upon request, give you a loose-leaf visa which should not be lost. Do not allow them to stamp your passport, or you will be banned from re-entry to the South. There is currently no limit on the number of times you may cross. EU citizens have the right of unrestricted movement throughout Cyprus; there may be restrictions for non-EU citizens, especially coming from North to South, though these may not be enforced.

Motorists going from South to North must buy supplemental insurance at the border, since no EU-contracted policies are valid in the Turkish Cypriot sector. The minimum term is 3 days, and the policies – with a scandalously low level of cover, and a record of not paying out compensation – are all but useless other than to wave at police. If you have an accident that immobilises you in the North, get the car moving again without involving the car-hire company in the South – do not risk being stranded in the North.

Fisherman at Keryneia

of water just offshore around 300 BC and was discovered in 1967 by a Greek-Cypriot diver. The surviving hull has been painstakingly preserved and remounted, and is shown with part of its final cargo.

In the foothills behind Keryneia are the substantial ruins of the superbly sited Gothic abbey of **Bellapais** 🐮 (Beylerbeyi; daily summer 9am–8pm, winter 9am–4.45pm). Facing the sea, the 'Abbaye de la Paix' (of which the current name is a corruption) stands on a 30-metre (100ft)-high escarpment, its buildings enveloped in cypresses, palms and citrus trees. The abbey was built by Premonstratensian (Norbertine) brothers generously funded by Lusignan kings, and took on its present form during the 13th and 14th centuries. The elegant cloister is adorned with finely carved figures, while the splendid vaulted refectory has six bays and a fine rose window; underneath the refectory is a fine undercroft with 'palm' vaulting upholding the ceiling.

West of Keryneia

You can follow the line of the Pentadaktylos range west to their end, and continue on through the main Maronite Catholic village of **Kormakitis** (Koruçam), enjoying something of a revival since 2003, with property being confidently renovated. Southward around the curve of Morfou Bay is the old bishop's seat of **Morfou** 🐮 (Mórphou/Güzelyurt) and its venerable monastery of **Agios Mamas** (daily summer 9am–7pm, winter 9am–4.15pm), one of the few churches in the North still used (on feast days) for Orthodox worship, thanks to the efforts of the charismatic Bishop of Morfou, Neophytos.

On the narrow strip of Northern Cyprus squeezed between the buffer zone and the sea lie the remains of the 6th-century BC Graeco-Roman town of **Soloi** ㊾ (Soli; daily summer 9am–6.45pm, winter 9am–4.45pm) and those of the Persian-era (5th-century BC) palace at **Vouni** (Vuni; daily summer 10am–5pm, winter 9am–4.45pm). Soloi is known for its fine mosaics, difficult to see except on bright days owing to a huge protective canopy.

Famagusta (Gazimağusa)

Bellapais Abbey

The east-coast port of **Famagusta** ㊿ (Ammochostos/Gazimağusa) was a mere village when Christian refugees arrived from Palestine in 1291. Soon it developed into a boom-town of extravagant merchants and notorious courtesans, becoming one of the wealthiest cities in the world. It all ended in late 1373 when the Genoese took the port as part of their general attacks across Cyprus. Worse was to come in 1571, with the Turkish invasion and the most famous siege in the island's history.

Famagusta emerged during the 20th century as the most important port in Cyprus and a major tourist centre. But once again, in 1974, a Turkish invasion was to leave the city a mere shadow of its former self. Since the departure of the Greek Cypriots, **Varosha** (Varosia/Varósha/Maraş), the pre-1974 beach resort area, is eerily deserted and decrepit. Yet the Venetian fortifications and old town are still of great interest.

Beside the harbour stands **Othello's Tower** (daily summer 9am–7pm, winter 9am–4.45pm), named after a 16th-century governor of Cyprus, Christoforo Moro, sometimes cited as the model for Shakespeare's tormented Moor. Most formidable of the fortifications is the **Martinengo Bastion** in the north-west corner of the old town. Its walls, 4–6 metres (13–19ft) thick, provided stubborn resistance to the Ottomans during the siege of 1570–1.

The town's many churches were founded by the Lusignans. The finest was St Nicholas' Cathedral, where the Lusignan kings were crowned honorifically as kings of Jerusalem. It was converted into a mosque, the **Lala Mustafa Paşa Camii** (daily dawn–dusk), named after the commander of the Ottoman siege. The handsome structure was completed in 1326 with a majestic western façade modelled on Rheims cathedral. Although the Turks stripped the interior of any images of the human form, and there was damage from an earthquake in 1735, it still retains fine Gothic features.

Othello's Tower, Famagusta

Salamis

Overlooking the sea just 8km (5 miles) north of Famagusta, the ancient city of **Salamis**

51 (daily summer 9am–7pm, spring/autumn 9am–6pm, winter 9am–1pm and 2–4.45pm) rivals Kourion (see page 56) as the island's finest archaeological site. For almost 1,800 years, Salamis competed with Paphos as the leading city in Cyprus and was a haven for exiled Greek artists and intellectuals. Renamed Constantia, it became the capital of early-Christian Cyprus in about AD 350, subsequently suffering an earthquake and the silting up of its port; the city was abandoned after the Arab invasions.

Converted from a cathedral, Lala Mustafa Paşa Mosque

The **Roman theatre** – tied for the largest in Cyprus, with the Nea Paphos theatre – seated 15,000. Also impressive is the spacious **gymnasium**. The graceful Corinthian columns of its **palaestra** were brought here from the theatre and re-erected by the Byzantines. In the adjoining **public baths**, you can distinguish the *frigidarium*, *tepidarium* and *caldarium* chambers. The water was channelled from Kythrea, 40km (25 miles) away, via a Roman aqueduct, parts of which are still standing. Check the ceiling vaults closely for superb mosaic fragments and frescoes, the latter clearly showing two figures reminiscent of Buddhist cave art.

Just west of Salamis is the monastery of **Apostolos Varnavas** **52** (daily summer 9am–7pm, winter 9am–1pm and 2–4.45pm). He accompanied Paul on his mission to Cyprus in AD 45 and was martyred in Salamis at the hands of Jews he was trying to convert. The saint's rock-cut subterranean burial chamber (free entry) is now empty, but its discovery in AD 478 helped the Church of Cyprus achieve autonomy within the Orthodox faith, and led to the building of the monastery nearby. The present drum-domed church was built in 1756 with elements from an earlier 15th-century church and columns and capitals from Salamis. It is now a museum of mediocre post-Byzantine icons; more worthwhile is an extensive archaeological gallery, the North's largest, in the building just behind.

The Karpasia Peninsula

By overnighting in the North, you'll be able to make a long, exhilarating drive into the 'panhandle' of the Karpasia (Karpaz) Peninsula. Don't try this on a day-trip – the distances are enormous and, despite improvements, the road network still too challenging.

The peninsula can be said to start at the castle of **Kantara** ❸, the easternmost and most intact of the Byzantine-Lusignan castles of the Pentadaktylos range (daily summer 9am–6pm, winter 9am–4.45pm). Even at its base, Karpasia is so narrow that the citadel was able to simultaneously survey both its north and south coasts. Tradition places the surrender of Isaac Komnenos to Richard the Lionheart here in 1191.

The main peninsular trunk road reaches the north coast just past Aigialousa (Yenierenköy); immediately after, in the village of **Agias Trias** ❺ (Sipahi), is a 5th-century **Christian basilica** with some of the finest floor mosaics on Cyprus, probably executed by the same craftsmen responsible for those at Kourion and Nea Paphos. They are mostly geometric, except for a peculiar motif of paired sandals – possibly symbolic of the journey through this world to the next.

Continue east to **Dip-karpaz (Rizokarpaso)** 🚌, Karpasia's largest village and a curiosity in that about 230 Greek Orthodox continue to live here; bypassed by the invasion, they were never forcibly expelled but did endure extremely hard times until 2003. There's food and lodging along the road between here and **Agios Filon (Ayfilon),** the site of ancient Karpasia, of which only a large, half-intact basilica, romantically flanked by palm trees, remains. A little west extends an excellent beach, known as **Dipkarpaz Halk Plajı**. Some 18km (11 miles) beyond is another stunning beach, Cyprus'

Sculpture in the ancient theatre at Salamis

best: **Nangomi** ('Golden Beach') 🚌, where rustic dune-top bungalows inland constitute the only real backpacker 'resort' on the island. You've probably seen 5,000-metre (3-mile)-long 'Golden Beach' already, as it figures in almost every northern Cypriot tourism promotional poster.

Last stop, near Karpasia's stormy tip, is the much-venerated monastery of **Apostolos Andreas** 🚌 (church open reasonable daylight hours). Despite free transit from the South for pilgrims since 2003, and a resident priest, the premises – tenanted by some elderly caretakers – are still visibly dilapidated, and there's still little sign of pending repair works funded by the UN and the USA.

WHAT TO DO

Cyprus offers plenty to do beyond sightseeing. Sporting activities benefit from a great climate and clear coastal waters, while entertainment ranges from some of the Mediterranean's hottest nightclubs in Agia Napa to more sedate dance presentations or concerts in an ancient open-air amphitheatre or vaulted medieval building.

SPORTS

Beaches may not all have the best sands, but they do have crystal-clear, unpolluted seas. Hikers can find solitude and marvellous scenery in the unspoilt Troödos and Pentadaktylos mountains, or on the rugged Akamas Peninsula.

Water Sports

Scuba divers and **snorkellers** are major beneficiaries of Cyprus' limpid seas. In water temperatures ranging from 16°C (60°F) to 27°C (80°F), you can explore submerged cliffs, valleys and caves, and get close-up views of sea anemones, sponges and crustaceans (although colourful fish are not abundant in the nutrient-poor eastern Mediterranean). You can also dive over several wrecks, best of all the ferry *Zenobia*, which sank off Larnaka in 1980. You will find certified diving centres with equipment for hire and instruction at Pafos, Coral Bay, Lakki, Larnaka, Limassol, Agia Napa and Protaras in the South, and at Keryneia (Girne) in the North. One particularly good outfitter for the *Zenobia* wreck is Larnaka- and Limassol-based Dive-In (tel: 24627469; www. dive-in.com.cy).

Parasailing off the beach at Agia Napa

Clear water allows for
great snorkelling

Windsurfing is widely
practiced, though conditions
are best around Cape Gkreko,
Pafos and Polis Bay; equipment can be hired at public
and hotel beaches. **Jet-skiing**
and **parasailing** are available at the main resorts.
Those serious about **sailing**
can hire craft from the har-
bours at Agia Napa, Pafos,
Lakki, Larnaka, Limassol and
Keryneia.

Golf

Golf is not a game much associated with Cyprus, but five excellent courses in the South are worth seeking out: **Secret Valley**,
tucked away not far from Petra tou Romiou; **Aphrodite Hills**
close by; **Tsada**, northeast of Pafos; and **Vikla** and **Elias** near
Limassol. The North has courses at Pentageia (Yeşilyurt) and
Agios Amvrosios (Esentepe).

Walking, Hiking and Jeep Safaris

The Troödos Mountains and Akamas Peninsula are ideal for
hiking, though for most people it will be too uncomforta-
ble in summer. The Cyprus Tourism Organisation has maps
and information on local itineraries (see page 134). Visit
the Pafos or Polis offices for the Akamas Peninsula, and the
Pano Platres office for the Troödos Mountains. Ask at any
CTO office for the excellent *Nature Trails* brochure, which
maps out walks all over the south of the island. Adjacent
to the Baths of Aphrodite car park, there's a CTO placard
that has details of walking trails; from here paths lead off
into the Akamas – with the exception of the unmissable

traverse of the Avgas (Avakas) Gorge, reached from the peninsula's southwest shore. In the North, the Pentadaktylos Mountains look tempting, but few proper trails exist – only jeep tracks.

The most popular nature trails in the Troödos are the Atalante and Artemis ones around Mt Olympos, and the shorter hikes up to Kaledonia Falls or out to Makrya Kontarka along the Persephone trail, but better and more unspoilt is the loop route around Madari (Madhári) ridge, with the most accessible trailhead (and best parking) near Kyperounta (Kyperoúnda).

Jeep safaris into the Akamas region and the Pafos foothills, pioneered by now-defunct Exalt Travel, have become much of a muchness and indeed no new licenses for operators are being given, owing to their environmental destructiveness as carried out by most outfitters. For a more sensitive, entertaining and knowledgeable custom tour, visiting areas few outsiders ever see, contact Pafos-based licensed guide David Pearlman (tel: 99603513; email: taramas@cytanet.com.cy).

On Two Wheels

Fancy a spot of mountain-biking? Cyprus has the mountains, and you can hire bikes in all the main resorts. There's little to stop you – except the fact that the grades are dauntingly steep, it's going to be hot up there and the steed you're riding will probably look as if it went through Cyprus with Richard the Lionheart.

If you're sure you can hack it, there's plenty of testing dirt tracks in the Troödos and Pentadaktylos mountains, on the Akamas Peninsula, around Cape Gkreko and in the wilds of Tillyria, Pitsilia and Karpasia. Take plenty of water and don't overdo it in summer. Anyone of a less rugged disposition can content themselves with a relaxing cycle along the many quiet, paved and mostly flat minor roads close to the sea.

Horse Riding

There are a dozen reputable stables or riding clubs in the South, mostly around Limassol and Pafos, as horse riding (during the cooler months) has grown in popularity. The CTO's Travellers Handbook lists them all; one to single out for lovely foothill itineraries and well-cared-for mounts is Drapia Farm outside Kalavassos village (tel: 99437188). There is also a decent stable in the North, at Agios Epiktitos (Çatalköy).

Extreme Sports

You can augment the hazards of partying in Agia Napa with **bungee-jumping** at nearby Nissi Beach: the drop is 60 metres (200ft). The **Slingshot**, also in Agia Napa, claims to be the highest and fastest ride in the world. Riders are propelled to a height of 100 metres (300ft) in a breathtaking 1.3 seconds. **Tandem paragliding** is a spectacular option from the palisades of the hills above Keryneia (Girne).

SHOPPING

The quality of many tourist shops in Cyprus is low, tending towards cheap, imported tat. Head instead for the nearest **Cyprus Handicraft Service** (CHS) shop, showcasing the best of the island's artisans. Goods here are comparatively expensive, but they are handmade and have the CHS label to guarantee it. You will find CHS shops at – **Pafos**: Apostolou Pavlou 64; **Limassol**: Themidos 25; **South Nicosia**: CHS workshop, Leoforos Athalassis 186; **Larnaka**: Kosma Lysioti 6. You can also find the works of talented craftspeople in various fields in their own shops and in outlets that stock quality products.

The giftshops of many of the South's museums – in particular the Cyprus Museum in Nicosia, and the Pierides in Larnaka – have very covetable articles, in particular reproduction Byzantine/Lusignan ceramics. Subject to the import rules of your home country, don't overlook a range of distinctive Cypriot foodstuffs and drink.

Best Buys

Basketry. The choice ranges from small baskets or trays, *tsésti*, in decorative shapes and colours to large articles in rush or cane.

Ceramics. Most ceramics are crude and garish. Seek out artisans who look back to antiquity for inspiration, or who are genuinely avant garde. Quality workshops/showrooms are scattered through the old Turkish-Cypiot quarters of Larnaka and Limassol.

Colourful ceramic souvenirs

Copperware. After three millennia, the copper industry remains a source of Cypriot pride. There are all manner of hand-crafted wares, including pots, saucepans and bowls.

Embroidery. Fine linen tablecloths, doilies, runners and handkerchiefs, stitched with the intricate geometric patterns of *lefkarítika* from Lefkara, and the more colourful *pafítika* from Pafos.

Terracotta urns for sale

Food and wine. A sweet, jelly-like confection, *loukoúmi*, or 'Cyprus Delight', is a speciality of Geroskipou. The Turkish version, *lokum*, or 'Turkish Delight', is sold in the North. Well-sealed packets of *loúntza* (cured pork loin) travel well, as do carefully wrapped bottles of *teratzómelo* (carob syrup) – unbeatable on yoghurt, oatmeal or baked into muffins. Of the many wines and liqueurs produced in Cyprus, the most popular gift is the fortified red dessert wine Commandaria.

Icons. Pieces available range from exquisite works produced by highly skilled monastic artists, to the cheaper items on sale in most gift shops.

Jewellery. You can find good-quality silver and gold, but in the resorts quality can be poor. Unadulterated silver and gold articles must be hallmarked; learn what the hallmarks look like, and much more, at www.assay.org.cy.

Leather goods. Manufactured locally, shoes and sandals are reasonably priced in Cyprus.

ENTERTAINMENT

Most resorts have a tourist-office brochure or a privately produced publication listing what's on. Another excellent resource is website www.cyprusevents.net.

Folklore Shows

Many hotels offer weekly folklore shows with costumed performers singing and dancing to traditional Greek tunes. Visitors are encouraged to get up and dance along. Many tavernas also have Greek-Cypriot or Greek dancing on a regular basis.

In Northern Cyprus, you may find (and be invited to engage in) belly dancing, and can enjoy Turkish music from enthusiastic if not always terribly talented local combos.

Historic Venues

The most memorable and distinctive evening's entertainment on offer are those staged at ancient or medieval premises. The **Pafos Odeion** stages plays (in English), while the Fort is the venue for opera performances each September. **Kourion's** unimprovably set amphitheatre is a wonderful place to catch a Shakespeare play or classical drama, or to hear a live concert (usually in July). Hire a cushion or take one along to sit at the outdoor theatres. Increasingly, Cyprus' numerous acoustically excellent medieval buildings are being used as venues; don't miss the chance to hear a chamber concert in the refectory

Nightlife and Agia Napa

Agia Napa is one of the Mediterranean's major party destinations for clubbers, with options ranging from 1980s-revival nights to the latest sounds. In July and August the crowd is very much 18–30 and can get rowdy at times – if not downright homicidal. Agia Napa, sadly, is the South's murder capital, and almost every year sees a fatal incident. The authorities have long operated a zero tolerance policy towards drugs, which has sent many patrons to Ibiza or Zakynthos. Outside the high season, you will find older, more discerning tastes being catered for.

The trendiest clubs change annually, but places like Castle (http://the-castleclub.com) or Black N White seem able to keep up. Don't go out too early – the real action doesn't start until around 1am. Limassol and Nicosia also have respectable nightlife scenes, but Kato Pafos clubs are essentially over.

Rockpooling on Nissi Beach

of Bellapais Abbey, the under-croft of La Cavocle at Kouklia, or the Kasteliotisa hall in old Nicosia. Nearly as impressive are revamped 20th-century structures, like the Rialto Theatre in Limassol and the Shoe Factory or the Municipal Theatre in Nicosia.

CHILDREN'S CYPRUS

With clean beaches and end-less sunshine, Cyprus is great for children (but be sure to protect them from the fierce Mediterranean sun). Cypriots, like most southern Europeans, love children and there are few, if any, restrictions on where they can go.

If the kids are bored with the beach, but not with the water, there are four waterparks to experience. **WaterWorld**, just west of Agia Napa at Agia Thekla, claims to be the biggest in Europe, with over 20 Greek-mythology-themed rides, ranging from high-speed thrill chutes to the Lazy River. There are three other waterparks in the South: **Wet 'n' Wild**, just east of Limassol, is larger and wilder than **Watermania** at Fassouri. The **Paphos Aphrodite Waterpark** between Pafos and Geroskipou also has its superlatives, including a long rafting ride.

The biggest and best amusement park is **Paliatso Fun Fair Luna Park** in Agia Napa. Kids will also enjoy a chance to view the underwater world from a **glass-bottomed boat**, such as the 30-seat **Yellow Submarine**, which operates from Agia Napa.

Festivals and Holy Days

6 January *Ta Fota*. On Epiphany Day, bishops bless the waters in seaside towns, throwing a crucifix into the sea to be recovered by divers.

February/March *Carnival*. Limassol's 10-day long celebration features fancy-dress balls and a final-Saturday parade. It's not Rio, but it's fun.

April/May *Easter*. Good Friday eve sees solemn liturgies everywhere, following by the parading of the *Epitafios* (Christ's Bier) along main thoroughfares. The Saturday midnight *Anastasi* (Resurrection) service has the congregation lighting their candles from the priest's, followed by spectacular fireworks displays – and, in Pafos district, dangerous deployment of explosives removed from the now-defunct Limni mines. These often drown out the most beautiful church chanting, occurring after midnight. *Cyprus Film Days*. Ten-day festival of the best new European and Asian cinema, mostly at the Rialto Theatre in Limassol.

May *Pharos International Chamber Music Festival*. A week of top-drawer concerts at Nicosia's PASYDY Theatre and La Cavocle at Palaipaphos (www.thepharostrust.org).

May/June *Kataklysmos*. The Festival of the Flood coincides with Pentecost, and this two-day holiday harks back to ancient times, when Cypriots convened at temples to worship and sacrifice to Adonis and Aphrodite. Today, there are excursions to the beach, parties, games, colourful parades and competitions at all coastal towns.

June *Shakespeare Festival*. Performances at the Kourion amphitheatre.

July *Larnaka Summer Festival*. Music, dance and theatre performances staged at the castle and the Pattikhion Theatre. *Paradise Jazz Festival*. Two successive weekends of jazz at Paradise Place in Pomos.

15 August *Dormition of the Virgin*. The faithful gather in massive crowds at the leading monasteries and churches. After Easter, the most important day in the Greek religious calendar.

September *Limassol Wine Festival*. Twelve days of wine-tastings, dancing and folklore shows. *Ayia Napa International Festival*. Folklore, music, dance and theatre around the monastery. *Paphos Aphrodite Festival*. Several days of top-notch opera around the fort.

EATING OUT

The food of Cyprus will be familiar to anyone who has visited Greece (or, in the case of Northern Cyprus, Turkey). Basically, it comprises grilled meats and fish, salads and a small selection of speciality casseroles. Fresh vegetables, though grown in abundance on the island, don't always find their way on to restaurant tables.

At its best, Cypriot cooking is simple, hearty and healthy. Unfortunately, mass tourism has encouraged bland 'international cuisine', and worse still, mass catering has had a baleful effect on local eateries. Bright-pink factory-produced *taramosaláta* and imitation crab sticks are now passed off in some places as part of a traditional fish *mezé* (see page 101).

Where to Eat

Many tourist-orientated restaurants on the resort strips give fair warning of the fact with lurid picture-menus; if you are at all serious about your food, choose very carefully where you eat with the aid of our listings. There's no reason to accept inferior fare, as it's now a buyer's market – more than 100 restaurants, mostly dodgy ones, have gone bust in the Pafos area alone since 2011.

Most restaurants serve lunch noon–3pm, and dinner 6.30–11.30pm; a few (usually more tourist-orientated and/or beachfront) stay open all day. If you are set on a particular restaurant in low season, it's advisable to call ahead, as some places close early or fail to open at all in winter.

In Cyprus, the term *taverna* implies an informal, even rustic traditional eating and drinking establishment. Of late, the *maeirkó*, or casserole-food kitchen, cheaply dishing out full, home-style meals, is making a big comeback in the larger southern towns. Another type of eatery is the *mezé* house,

A classic Greek salad

known as a *meyhane* in the North. At these, there will often be no menu, just a fixed price for a set meal of the house specialities. In the North, a variant of this is 'full kebab', where relays of grilled titbits – sausage, kidneys, baby chops – are brought to your table piping hot.

Fast Food and Starters

Cypriot fast food generally means a *pita* bread stuffed with *sheftaliá/şeftalya* (a kind of sausage) or *souvláki/şiş kebap*, grilled cubes of fresh lamb or goat, plus garnish, and a yogurt dressing. The ingredients will be fresh and the *sheftaliá* home-made, with local herbs. You'll get these snacks at small takeaways or cafés.

Any starter section of a menu is likely to contain the following four dips: *taramosaláta/tarama*, a light pink fish-roe paste made with olive oil and lemon juice, and thickened with mashed potato or bread crumbs; *talatoúra/talatur*,

Dining in Nicosia old town

a Cypriot variant of the Greek *tzatzíki* (yoghurt with cucumber, crushed garlic and fresh mint); *tahíni/tahin*, a sesame-seed paste with garlic; and *hummus*, puréed chick-peas, olive oil and spices. To accompany these dips, you will usually be served *pita* bread, and *tsakistés/çakistes*, marinated split green olives.

Koupépia/yaprak dolması is another well-known starter – vine leaves stuffed with rice and lamb, flavoured with mint. Two more permanent items on the starter section of a menu are *loúntza*, a thinly sliced fillet of smoked pork, and *halloúmi/hellim*, a Cypriot ewe's- or goat's-milk cheese (sadly inferior cow milk-based formulas are common). Both of these will probably be served hot (chargrilled or fried), and are often offered as a combination. More commonly found in *mezé* medleys are *lougánigo/bumbar*, smoked sausage, *shiroméri* (another variety of cured pork), or *tsamarélla/samarella*, lamb (or even better) goat salami.

Soups are not common on menus (apart from vegetable soup, usually made from leftovers). But if you do get the chance, try *avgolémono/düğün*, a lemon-flavoured chicken broth thickened with egg and served with rice. Another rarity to look out for is *kypriakes ravioles/pirohu*, Cypriot ravioli stuffed with *halloúmi*, eggs and mint.

Main Dishes and Vegetables

Almost without exception, resort restaurants have a section on their menus entitled 'Cypriot Specialities'. This typically includes: *moussaká/musaka*, a layered dish of minced meat, aubergine and potatoes, with bechamel sauce topping and spices; *afélia*, a tender pork stew made with red wine, cumin and coriander seeds; *kléftigo/küp kebap*, oven-roasted lamb or goat, the traditional Sunday lunch for the locals; *davás/dava*, a sweetish, onion-laden, clay-pot stew, usually of lamb; and *keftédes/köfte*, meat balls flavoured with herbs, usually coriander and cumin. Less common but well worth trying are *ortíchia/bıldırcın*, roast quail, or *koúppes*, torpedo-shaped fried turnovers stuffed with onions and mincemeat.

In tourist areas, everything is served with French fries unless you specify rice or the healthy *pourgoúri/bulgur* (cracked wheat), which Cypriots adore. 'Village' salad means

Mezé

Mezé – pronounced as written, not 'metze' as Anglophones tend to do – is the designation for the relays of small speciality platters brought to your table in the better Cypriot standard tavernas and dedicated *mezé* houses/*meyhanes*. The portions may be small, but the platters – usually 20 to 25 of them, mixing appetisers and larger servings of main courses – add up to a meal and a half. This makes an excellent crash course in Cypriot food and is usually good value, though invariably it must be ordered by a minimum of two people. The choice is usually between meat *mezé* or fish *mezé*, though of late vegetarian *mezé* is also offered. It is a bad sign (and considered disgusting by Cypriots) for an establishment to offer a mixed meat-seafood *mezé*. Any type of *mezé* is likely to contain exotic vegetarian elements, such as *kouloúmbra* (kohlrabi), an excellent palate-cleanser; *moúngra* (pickled cauliflower); *kappára/kappa* (whole pickled caper plants); and oyster mushrooms (*plevrótous*), which grow on fennel roots.

a bowl of lettuce or cabbage, cucumber, tomatoes, possibly olives and always a thick slice or two of *feta* cheese; better chefs will include rocket, coriander greens, purslane or parsley in the mix.

In more authentic restaurants, you should be able to get *louviá/bürülce* (black-eyed peas) or, in springtime, fresh *goutsiá/bakla* (broad beans), both served with just lemon or vinegar and oil without sauce. Cheese-stuffed eggplant is another frequent treat, as is *bámies/bamya* (okra, lady fingers). More arcane, home-style specialities are *kolokássia/bules*, taro root, introduced to the island long ago, often stewed together with meat or chicken; and *molehíya/molohiya*, a mint-like plant from Egypt, served by itself or more frequently stewed with meat, especially in the North.

Fish and Shellfish

As offshore catches get scantier, the choice of seafood becomes more limited and prices increase accordingly. Most seafood in the South is either frozen, farmed, imported, or all three, and menus may be reticent on the subject. It's widely acknowledged that the best fresh fish on the island is to be found along the northern Karpasia Peninsula. Octopus (*khtapódi/ahtapod*) is served in a red wine sauce, or grilled. Prawns (*karídes/karides*) or battered squid (*kalamarákia/kalamar*) are other common menu items.

Octopus salad

The commonest fresh, non-farmed fish include *lagós/lahoz* (small grouper), common bream (*sorkós/sargoz*), bogue (*wóppes/woppa*), red mullet *(parpoúni/tekir)*, amberjack *(mayátiko/mineri)* and whitebait *(marídes/smirida)*. Large fish is usually simply barbecued, smaller species flash-fried. The speciality of the Troödos Mountains is farmed trout, fried or grilled.

Desserts and Sweets

Dessert usually means a small plate of fruit. Depending on the season, you'll be able to try the island's outstanding loquats, strawberries, guavas, citrus, grapes, figs, watermelon, Persian melons, plums and cherries. Another possibility is *glyká/macun*, preserved candied fruits or even

Oranges ready for picking

vegetables – which can mean Seville oranges and green walnuts.

The popular oriental sweets are rarely offered as dessert after a meal, but are served separately in cafés. Honey and nuts are used in both *baklavás/baklava*, layered filo pastry, and *kataïfi/kadayıf*, filaments resembling shredded wheat. Less cloyingly sweet and more genuinely Cypriot are *palouzé* (grape must pudding) and *mahallebí/muhallebi* (cherry-pit flour and rosewater pudding).

Coffee

The traditional local coffee is generic oriental style, served sweet *(glykó/şekerli)*, medium-sweet *(métrio/orta)*, or without sugar *(skéto/sade)*, accompanied by a glass of cool water. Do not disturb or drink the thick sediment at the bottom of the cup. Instant coffee – referred to as Nescafé irrespective of brand – has made massive inroads both North and South. Better establishments offer some kind of filter coffee, often Rombouts or Jacobs brand, and most self-catering villas provide a percolator machine for which packaged grounds are readily found at the nearest supermarket. Decent espresso, lattes or cappuccino are widely available at cafés in all the South's major towns; in the North you will only find properly made ones at certain locations in Nicosia, Famagusta and Keryneia – elsewhere it will be 'instant' espresso out of an envelope.

Wines

Cypriot wines have been known and enjoyed since ancient times. Most famous of them is the fortified red dessert wine Commandaria, originally produced for the Knights of St John at Kolossi, similar to Madeira and worth trying even if you don't normally like sweet wines. The biggest wineries produce sweet and dry sherry-type wines – ETKO Emva is reckoned the best of these.

By western Mediterranean standards, the quality of Cypriot table wines from the major wineries is often low, and a few are effectively undrinkable. It is always worth paying a bit more for a quality microwinery bottling, of which there are large numbers. Some of the most reliable include Constantinou at Pera Pedi, Tsiakkas in Pelendri, Tsangaridis in Lemona, Domaine Nicolaides in Anogyra, Fikardos in Mesogi and Vouni in Panagia. In the North, all wine is imported from Turkey with the exception of products of a single microwinery, Chateau St Hilarion.

Other Alcoholic Drinks

As an after-dinner drink, you may be offered a *zivanía*, the local fire water. Distilled from grape-pressing residue, it is similar to Cretan *rakí*. The best commercial brand is LOEL (45 percent alcohol). Mainland-Greek *ouzo*, a clear aniseed-flavoured spirit that turns milky with the addition of water, is also popular on Cyprus. In the North, the closest analogue (though stronger than *ouzo*) is *raki*, imported from Turkey; the best brands are Efe and Burgaz, green-label grade.

If you are going to drink Cypriot brandy straight, go for one of the better-known labels like Peristiany VO 31 or KEO Five Kings. Brandy is more commonly used as the base for a brandy sour (mixed with lemonade and bitters), the traditional island sundowner.

The local Southern beers are the pilsener Keo, or the lagers Carlsberg and its hoppier stablemate Leon. Beer in the North means Turkish Efes or the Austrian Gold Fassl lager brewed locally under licence. No island beer exceeds 5 percent alcohol content. Bars, but not restaurants, stock plenty of imports.

Cypriot wines have been appreciated since antiquity

FOOD NAMES

We give the Greek-Cypriot/Turkish-Cypriot names for foods in local dialect, which often varies sharply from the name in Greece. Sometimes a food is found only in one of the two communities; sometimes it's called the same North and South.

TO HELP YOU ORDER...

Could we have a table? **Boroúme na éhoume éna trapézi?**
I'd like a/an/some... **Tha íthela...**

I'm a vegetarian **Íme hortofágos**	butter **voútyro**
The bill, please **To logariazmó, parakaló**	salt **aláti**
	black pepper **mávro pipéri**
plate **piáto**	Cheers! **Giámas!**
cutlery **maheropírouna**	Bon appetit! **Kalí órexi!**
glass **potíri**	Good continuation!
bread **psomí**	(to the next course)
	Kalí synéhia!

MENU READER

fried **tiganitó**	rice **rýzi, piláfi**
baked **sto foúrno**	A litre/half litre **Éna kiló/ misó kilo**
roasted **psitó**	
grilled **sta kárvouna**	wine **krasí**
stuffed **gemistá**	beer **býra**
fish **psári**	mineral water **metallikó neró**
meat **kréas**	
beef **moskhári, vodinó**	coffee **kafés**
pork **hirinó**	filter coffee **kafés fíltrou**
goat **katsíki**	tea **tsái**
chicken **kotópoulo**	milk **gala**
lamb **arní**	sugar **záhari**
salad **saláta**	dessert **glykó, epidórpio**
aubergine/eggplant **melitzána**	fruit **froúta**
potatoes **patátes**	ice cream **pagotó**

PLACES TO EAT

We have used the following symbols to give an idea of the per-person price for a three-course meal (or a mezé), excluding drinks:

€€€€ over 40 euros   €€€ 25–40 euros

€€ 15–25 euros   € below 15 euros

SOUTHERN CYPRUS

NICOSIA

Kathodon €€ *Lidras 62D, tel: 22661656.* Open daily from noon until late. Just 100 metres/yds from the checkpoint, this place is enduringly popular with trendy Cypriots and discerning foreigners. The menu is Cypriot and mainland Greek fusion, either *mezé* format or à la carte, though wine choice is limited. Seating is on the ground floor, on a small loft or outside; satirical maxims and photos of film/music stars line the walls. There's quality acoustic Greek music most nights, and you have to book at weekends; come for the buzz as much as for the grub.

Pantopoleio €€€ *Vassileos Pavlou 7, tel: 22675151.* Open Mon–Sat for lunch and dinner. Since 2010, this taverna has gained a loyal following for fare straddling metropolitan Greek and Cypriot in the best possible way. Heaping salads or starters like stuffed breaded mushrooms, *ospriáda* (bean salad) or stuffed red Florina peppers precede mains such as pork chops garnished with eggplant purée. Save room for decadent desserts like mousse with orange zest, or rose-petal jam in a crumble crust. Pavement tables are always packed during warm weather; the 1920s interior, tricked out in homage to its past as a grocery (*pandopolío*), can get noisy.

Sawa €€ *Klimentos 31, Agios Antonios district, new town, tel:* 22766777. Open daily 1pm–late. One of two excellent Syrian restaurants in the capital, Sawa is popular with families who know good value when they see it. If the kitsch interior is too much, dine out in the garden (where a heated tent is erected in winter). It would be masochistic to have mains, when the *mezé*/salad platters are so rich – loaded with *nakanek* (sausage), fattoush (salad made with fried pita), tabbouli and *sodat dajaj* (chicken livers) among others. For dessert, try *mahallebí* or *baklavás*, neither overly sweet or gooey. For tipple, there's *arak* or *ouzo* to any measure, cheaper than the still-competitive wine list. Private parking is a plus in this congested area.

Zanettos €€ *Trikoúpi 65, old town, tel: 22765501, www.zanettos. com*. Open Tue–Sun for dinner, Tue–Sat for lunch. A modest entrance leads to this arcaded warren, going since 1938, with wall photos of past illustrious patrons staring down at you (except in the inside summer patio). Despite its fame among foreigners, quality has been maintained, with a loyal local following. They tuck into a monstrously large set-price *mezé*, which may include snails, wine-marinated spare ribs, sliced liver, bean dishes, and *pourgoúri* (bulgur wheat) with noodles; dessert (if you've room) comprises *mahallebí*, fruit and *halvás*. The Pafos bulk wine is decent.

LARNAKA

Art Cafe 1900 €€ *Stasinou 6, tel: 24653027*. Open daily 7pm–midnight. This charming bar-restaurant occupies a lovely early 20th-century townhouse near the Pierides Museum. Downstairs, among film posters on the walls, Marios offers the island's largest selection of beers (especially Belgian) and whiskies, plus expertly segued classic rock (he's a DJ by day). Upstairs, Maria presides over the Mediterranean-fusion restaurant, featuring dishes like chicken with orange juice, thyme and garlic; duck on special occasions; and vegetarian options. Wall décor consists of original canvases (Maria's and other artists'), while there may be apple crumble à la mode for dessert.

Gevseis en Lefko €€ *Piyale Paşa 8, tel: 99435963*. Open Tue–Sun for lunch and dinner. The name means 'tastes in white', and indeed the interior is all-white save for film-star photos and blue-checked tablecloths. The place styles itself a *mezedotavernío*, falling somewhere between a traditional tavern and a Greece-style *ouzeri*. Salads are copious, starters like baby aubergine stuffed with cheese and mince are first rate, but meat dishes are apt to disappoint compared to seafood like grilled octopus. Drink is reasonably priced.

Glykolemono € *Zinonos Kitieos 105, tel: 24623010.* Open daily 8am–8pm. Larnaca's favourite, and classiest, café, with Belle Epoque floor tiles but otherwise contemporary décor. Besides expertly brewed coffees, the stock in trade is speciality pastries like *peinirlí* and sweet or savoury *bougátsa* (custard pie), a great breakfast. Expensive for what it is; takeaway is much cheaper.

Zephyros €€–€€€ *Piyale Paşa 37, tel: 24657198.* Open Tue–Sun for lunch and dinner. The most reliably performing of several fish tavernas along here, with a tellingly high level of local patronage. Scaly fish or cephalopods come with the traditional *tsayíri* garnish rather than a formal salad: in springtime, probably celery, *kouloúmbra*, raw artichokes, lettuce, parsley and rocket. An army of black-and-white-liveried waiters provides efficient service.

AGIA NAPA AND REGION

Demetrion €€–€€€ *Limanaki, Potamos Liopetriou, tel: 23991010.* Open all year for lunch and dinner except Christmas/Easter. The more seaward of the two tavernas here, the smell of fresh fish and hand-cut chips frying in fresh oil tells you you've come to the right place. Avoid the cheaper seafood 'portions', which tend to be farmed species; go for by-weight offerings, which are really likely to be landed at the adjacent anchorage. Seating inside or out on the terrace, by season; it's a pleasantly breezy spot when the rest of the island is baking. Service is civil and fairly efficient despite habitual Cypriot crowds.

Markos €€–€€€ *Limanaki harbourfront, officially Makariou 44, Agia Napa, tel: 23721877.* Open March–November daily for lunch and dinner. The best value – at this resort, anyway – for wild fish by the kilo, such as *sorkós* (bream), *parpoúni* (red mullet) and *kourkoúna* (leatherback). Accompanying chips are fresh-cut, while side salads come with an accent of caper sprigs – confirm that these are included in the quoted price. Outdoor seating overlooks the open sea, not the little port.

Mastr-Antonis (Kamaskas) **€€€** *Daidalou 23, Paralimni; from CYTA roundabout, take the road towards Cape Gkreko and make the first right, tel: 23825144*. Open daily for lunch and dinner most of the year. This minimally signposted, Cypriot-favoured taverna is best in winter or spring, when seasonal delicacies like agrélia (asparagus) with eggs, wild mushrooms, fresh fish and game platters join usual offerings like lamb liver, mussel risotto and heaping salads. Both à la carte and mezé options are available, and there's a well-stocked cellar of Greek and Cypriot microwinery labels. The light stone-clad interior is more inspiring than the narrow terrace outside – another good reason to come off-season.

Ploumin **€€** *Ikosiogdois Oktovriou 3, Sotira, tel: 99658333, www. ploumin.com.cy*. Open daily summer for lunch and dinner, winter dinner only. Well-signed in the village centre, this listed building from 1938 features a double-arched interior with lithographs, old film stills, posters and pottery as décor, while old tools stand out in the summer patio. The mezé changes seasonally – interesting items like kolokássia (taro root) with lamb, zalatína (pork brawn) or fennel mushrooms may be 'off' – but rabbit is usually available. Bulk wine is from Statós village, or there's a well-stocked cellar of bottled choices. Live music two nights weekly.

LIMASSOL (LEMESOS) AND REGION

Dino Art Café, **€€€** *Irinis 62–66, old marketplace tel: 25762030*. Open Mon–Sat. Spearheading the revival of the old town since opening in 2006, Dino's vast fusion menu encompasses *wakami* salad, duck pate, carpaccio, a full range of sushi, jerk chicken, cheese platters, various pasta dishes and decadent desserts. Drinks include fresh-squeezed juices/smoothies, and pricey cocktails. The wall art, by local artists, is for sale and changes regularly.

Limanaki **€€€** *Pissouri beach, tel: 25221288, www.limanakipissouri.com*. Open daily for lunch and dinner except Dec to mid-

Feb. Middle Eastern, Indian and French accents to the fare here reflect proprietor-chef Sam Kazazz's Lebanese origins and Parisian training. The menu changes annually, but expect dishes like smoked duck salad, garlic mushrooms, cheese-stuffed chicken fillet, braised lamb shank, vegetarian tajine, makdous (cured, stuffed aubergines) or spring rolls. There's a full dessert list as well. Sit outside on the small terrace, or inside (where an 18-seater loft is ideal for private functions).

Sykaminia € *Eleftherias 26, old quarter,* tel: 25365280. Open Mon–Sat for lunch. A mid-2000s refurbishment hasn't dented the charm of this much-loved *maeirkó,* where archival photos of old Limassol adorn the walls. The menu stresses a few meat stews, simple fish fries like *marída,* and *óspria* (legume dishes), for which every table has a few onions (the usual garnish) poised at the ready. Fresh *goutsiá* (broad beans) with greens and celery are very good indeed. Bulk wine is surprisingly pricey.

Syrian Arab Friendship Club €€–€€€ *Iliados 3, opposite the Appolonia Beach Hotel, Potamos Germasogias tourist district,* tel: 25328838. Open daily noon–11.30pm. All the Syrian/Lebanese favourites are present and correct here: *mouhamara* (red pepper and walnut dip), *nakanek* sausages, *kibbeh* (bulgur wheat turnovers), *moutabhal* (aubergine dip). There's an à la carte menu, but two diners or more should opt for the famous *mezé* of 15 to 38 platters, according to party size. There are also three grades of *arak, zivanía, ouzo* and wine to drink. Sit by preference in the lovely garden fronted by a kitsch rendition of the Palmyra ruins (your clue that you've found the place); the interior is rather dull, though there are *shishas* on offer, toked on by single Arabic males, and loud music at weekends. Branches in Nicosia (Vassilisis Amalias 17, tel: 22776246) and Kato Pafos (Pafias Afroditis 14, tel: 26600278).

TROÖDOS MOUNTAINS

Ariadni € *Vasa, south of the village near bypass road,* tel: 25944064. Open daily for lunch and dinner, closed Tue in low season. A reliable, friendly outlet for homestyle fare like *koupépia* with sheep-milk yoghurt, *louviá* (black-eyed peas) with celery, *bourékia* (turnovers) stuffed with soft *anarí* cheese, and a couple of daily surprises. Wine is either in bulk, slightly sweet, or bottled products of the local winery. Success has prompted the opening of a winter annexe downhill, but the original fieldstoned premises are preferable.

Tziellari €€€ *Old Kakopetria 72, tel: 22922522.* Open summer daily for lunch and dinner, winter Thur–Sun. 'Tziellari' is Cypriot dialect for 'cellar', and you'll sit in a cosy one here during cooler months, but deserved success has prompted expansion to a front veranda and summer roof terrace. The fare is hybridised Argentine-Cypriot: ex-UN peacekeeper Victor mans the grill, whose products come topped with his secret green herbal sauce, but don't overlook starters like *empanadas* and grilled mushrooms. Wife Georgia commands the front of house; the wine list is mixed Argentine, Greek and Cypriot, plus there's Argentine Quilmez beer.

PAFOS AND REGION

Imogen's Inn €€ *Kathikas village centre, tel: 26633269.* Open Thur–Tue for dinner and often lunch, closed Nov–Feb. The menu offered by Marina, her Greek husband Apostolos and Marina's mum Eleni has Egyptian (for example foul madamas, mashed fava beans) and abundant mainland Greek inluences (Cretan dákos salad, saganáki, stuffed cabbage, stuffed red Florina peppers), reflecting the family history and make-up. The mains – including Eleni's daily special – are gut-busting; most diners will be happy with the mezé platters. Tables are in the rear patio, or the pastel-hued interior where a fire crackles in early spring.

Kouppas Stone Castle € *Neo Chorio (Neokhorió) village centre, tel: 26322526.* Open daily all day, as it doubles as village café. Your best option before or after a hike in the adjacent Akamas wilderness, with reasonably priced fish soup, *afélia*, *sheftaliá*, *kléftigo*, rabbit stew or roast chicken served in a pleasant, stone-clad diner, with *kataifi* or crème caramel for dessert. The owner Andreas has commendably resisted the blandishments of tour companies to provide low-quality meals for €5 a head to groups.

Laona € *Votsi 6, Ktima (Upper Pafos), tel: 26937121.* Open Mon–Sat 10am–4pm plus two variable evenings high season. This classic, very friendly marketplace maeirkó, inside a 1900-vintage interior (plus outdoors in summer), purveys such favourites as bean dishes, baked fish, rabbit stew, kolokássia with pork, plus desserts like palouzé and kalopráma (yoghurt, semolina and citrus zest pie). The quaffable bulk wine is from Statós village.

Sardegna di Gino €€ *Apostolou Pavlou 70, Shops 5–7, Kato Pafos, tel: 26933399.* Open Wed–Mon for dinner. The gay colour scheme announces you're about to scoff the island's best, wood-fired pizzas, courtesy of transplanted Sardinians Gino and Lisa. Be warned – on the menu 'small' means medium by most standards, 'medium' means large. There are giant salads, a short dessert list and Italian bulk or bottled wine. Eat indoors or out by season – or wherever there's space (booking suggested).

Seven St Georges €€€ *Anthypolohagou Georgiou M Savva 37, west edge of Geroskipou, tel: 99665824.* Open Tue–Sun for lunch and dinner. George Demetriades, now assisted by his sons Ben and Damian, offers what could well be the widest-ranging *mezé* on the island. All the ingredients are either organically grown or gathered wild by George; seasonally variable platters might include flash-fried *agrélia* (wild asparagus), goat-and-cumin *tavás*, sautéed wild *púngalos* greens, *tsamarélla* (goat), fried or pickled mushrooms and *kléftigo*. The quality of the food, the service and the old-house atmosphere, helped along by carefully selected Greek music, are a world away from the anonymous *kalamári*-and-chips joints of Kato Pafos. Wine, dessert and coffee are charged separately, bumping it into the higher price category.

Ta Perix €€ *Kioubilay 20, Moutallou district, Ktima (Upper Pafos), tel: 99539209.* Open Mon–Sat for dinner. The town's best mezé house, where you tick off choices from a proffered order form: quail eggs, agrélia, tyrokafterí (Greek spicy cheese dip), grilled quail, chicken livers, boiled greens, mushrooms. Those bored of being force-fed like a paté goose even get to specify the size of platter (small or large). It's justifiably popular, with a small interior, so weekend reservations are mandatory.

NORTHERN CYPRUS

NORTHERN NICOSIA (LEFKOŞA)

Müze Dostlar € *Lusignan chapter house, Selimiye Meydanı 35, tel: (392) 228 9345.* Open Mon–Sat noon–5pm. Anywhere else in Cyprus it would be a tourist trap, but this welcoming canteen – run by the Friends of the North Cyprus Museums – is the real deal. Tuck into homestyle dishes like *molohiya* stew or chicken with *kolokasa*, washed down by beer, *ayran* or sodas. It's okay to just stop by for a coffee; choose between a table out by the ex-cathedral's flying buttresses, or inside the magnificent medieval interior.

Sabor Latino €€ *Selimiye Meydanı 29, tel: 97620983, (392) 228 8322.* Open daily from 9am until late. This sleek coffee bar/bistro is somewhat misnamed now that its menu includes various Asian specials like spicy prawn soup, noodles with spinach and mushrooms and beef-vegetable stir-fry, all in hefty portions, alongside the prior tapas and Italian platters. There's a full list of decadent western desserts, alcoholic drinks despite the mosque opposite, and top-flight waiting service. This was the first place in the North to prepare decent espressos and cappuccinos, and continues to do so. Seating indoors or out, the latter with eyefuls of the Selimiye.

KERYNEIA (GIRNE) AND REGION

Archway €€ *Dereboyu Sok 5, Templos (Zeytinlik) village centre, 3km (2 miles) from Keryneia, tel: (392) 816 0353.* Open daily summer for lunch and dinner, winter dinner only. The best venue for carnivores in the area, served in tastefully mock-rustic surroundings. Choose between full kebab or various à la carte platters; mains should include side salad, yoghurt, chips and coffee, though not of course the French wine list (bulk wine is acceptable).

Lagoon €€€ *Kordonboyu 11, tel: (392) 815 6555.* Open most days for lunch and dinner. Lagoon has been the best seafood tavern in town for a number of years now, and the upper-deck, bay-view tables decorated with proper table linen are simply unbeatable. Choose between seafood *mezé* – a modest dozen platters – or wild-caught fish by the kilo, accompanied by rocket salad and grilled *hellim*. Products of the St Hilarion microwinery are also featured.

FAMAGUSTA (GAZİMAĞUSA)

Gingko €€ *Medrese (Koranic academy) next to Lala Mustaf Paşa,* tel: (392) 366 6660. Open daily 10.30am–midnight. The setting alone – under medieval domes and arches – would repay a visit, but the food quality, for salads and grills (and prices) very nearly matches that of Nicosia's Sabor Latino. It's fine to have just a coffee and a dessert.

KARPASIA (KARPAZ)

Alevkayalı €€–€€€ *Aytherisso Orthodox shrine, beyond Aigaialousa (Yenierenköy),* tel: (533) 876 0911. 'Taste the Sunset', says their business card – lots of people do, along with some of the best, and best-priced, fish in the North. Typical species include orfoz (grouper), sokan (leatherback), gilthead bream, and sorkoz. Mains orders include a small side salad and mini-mezé, with coffee also on the house.

Manolyam €€ *Rizokarpaso (Dipkarpaz), north neighbourhood,* tel: (392) 372 2209. This is the peninsula's only meyhane, with jolly, multi-ethnic, multilingual staff and five-platter mini-mezé included with any main course order (these most often tend to be stews). It's all served up in premises with Cypriot (rather than Turkish) folkloric décor.

Tuzlu Kuyu (Almyrolakkos) €€ *Alymrólakkos cove,* tel: (533) 844 1392. Unusually for the North, a Greek-Cypriot-run seafood taverna that does a good job of fish with chips and a mini-mezé; because of owner Nikos, it gets groups of pilgrims en route to Agios Andreas monastery, but service (by Kurdish waiters!) copes well.

A–Z TRAVEL TIPS

A Summary of Practical Information

A

ACCOMMODATION (also see page 137)

For high season (mid-June to October) stays, book well in advance for the place of your choice. The Cyprus Tourism Organisation (see page 134) produces a large pamphlet listing all licensed hotels and other types of accommodation. Failing that, you can find the same information on the CTO's website, www.visitcyprus.com, through the 'Accommodation' tab. The North Cyprus tourist board also publishes an annual guide to accommodation, but this proves less than exhaustive.

> I'd like a single/double room **Tha íthela éna monóklino/ díklino**
> What's the rate per night? **Póso stihízei giá mía nýkhta?**

Hotels. Cyprus has hotels in all categories, from five-star luxury havens and comfortable guest-houses to pleasant hotel-apartments in three grades. All-inclusive resorts, especially around Pafos, are beginning to multiply. All hotels offer discounts during low season, which for seaside resorts is from November to March, and for hill resorts from October to June – both excluding the Christmas/New Year and Easter weeks. Many beach hotels close from New Year to the end of March.

Villas. Self-catering villas are most numerous around Pafos and Keryneia, with lesser numbers in the Limassol foothills and around Larnaka. They are best rented through our recommended agencies (see below).

Agrotourism. Through a CTO initiative, many traditional houses in the countryside have been renovated and are now rented out as holiday homes. For details, secure a copy of the booklet *Cyprus Agrotourism: A Guide to Traditional Holiday Homes*, or access their website, www.agrotourism.com.cy, which also has a booking facility.

Recommended package operators. For the South, Sunvil (www.sunvil.co.uk) has the best selction of villas and agrotourist facilities, plus selected hotels; Libra Holidays (www.libraholidays.co.uk) is more mid-market. For the North, Green Island Holidays (www.green-islandholidays.com) are specialists, with a wide range of resort hotels; Anatolian Sky (www.anatolian-sky.co.uk) are Keryneia area specialists.

AIRPORTS

Larnaka International Airport (LCA; tel: 77778833; www.cyprus airports.com.cy), Cyprus' principal air gateway, lies 5km (3 miles) from Larnaka town and 50km (30 miles) from Nicosia. Dedicated airport shuttles run frequently between the airport and Pafos, Limassol (www.airportshuttlebus.eu) and Nicosia (www.kapnosairport shuttle.com). Only expensive private transfers are available for Agia Napa and Protaras. Several urban buses operate daily to Larnaka. A daytime taxi fare is about €10.

Pafos International Airport (PFO; tel: 77778833; www.cyprus airports.com.cy), 11km (7 miles) southeast of Pafos on the west coast, handles several no-frills airlines and many charter services. Local buses run frequently between the airport and Pafos. Daytime taxi fares range from €30 to the centre of Pafos up to €60 to Limassol, for which www.airportshuttlebus.eu is a better option.

Ercan International Airport (ECN; tel: (392) 231 4806; www.ercan airport.co.uk) in Northern Cyprus, 14km (9 miles) east of Nicosia, is served by UK-originating flights which must stop in Turkey en route. There is a limited shuttle-bus service to Keryneia, north Nicosia and Famagusta. Taxis serve all points in the North, expensively.

B

BICYCLE AND MOTORCYCLE HIRE

You can hire bikes and motorcycles in all important southern resorts, though motorbike hire is overpriced and thus not popular,

especially given local car-driver habits. You must be at least 18 years
of age and hold the correct licence; 17-year-olds may hire a moped
of maximum 49cc. Crash helmets must be worn by both driver and
pillion passengers; reputable agencies supply them.

Mountain biking, particularly in the Troödos or Pentadaktylos
(Beşparmak) mountains, and on the Akamas Peninsula, is popular
but strenuous. Cycling along coastal back roads is far easier. The
CTO (see page 134) has a brochure, *Cyprus for Cycling* (hard copy or
download through www.visitcyprus.com), detailing 19 routes. For
more details, contact the Cyprus Cycling Federation; tel: 22449870,
www.cypruscycling.com.

BUDGETING FOR YOUR TRIP

Pricewise, Cyprus is above average as a Mediterranean destination – more expensive than most Greek islands, Turkey, much of
Spain and southern Portugal, about the same as provincial France,
but cheaper than Italy. In high season, airfares from Britain cost
around £200–300 and a good four-star hotel room will be about
€150 per night. For the North, airfares are about the same, though
lodging costs somewhat less. Booking a package, particularly at
the last minute, will save you money; see our agency recommen-
dations above.

Food and drink across the island is moderate (a three-course meal
without drinks in a simple restaurant usually costs about €17–25 per
person). Drinks in bars and restaurants range from €3.50 for a beer
in a simple place to €10 and over for cocktails in a fancy establishment. Wine is relatively expensive in the North. Museum entry is
generally inexpensive, ranging from under a euro to €4.

C

CAR HIRE (see also Driving)

As many sights in Cyprus are spread out, and beyond the reach of public transport, it is worth hiring a car. To hire a car in the South, you must have a valid national driver's licence (held for at least three years) or, for non-EU nationals, an International Driving Permit. Depending on the company, the minimum age is 21 to 25. A deposit is usually required, payable by credit card. Check whether driving on unsurfaced roads will invalidate the insurance.

The most effective way of booking a car in advance is via a consolidator website like www.comparecarrentals.co.uk, www.auto-europe. co.uk/autoeurope-com, or www.skycars.co.uk. Rates, always with unlimited mileage, begin as low as €8 per day for the smallest compact in winter, more than doubling in summer. For a decent family-sized car, plan on spending €35 per day in high season. If you do not have an annual CDW insurance policy (these are well worth it if you hire cars more than two weeks annually; try www.insurance4carhire. com), you'll need to add another few euros per day. In summer, air-conditioning is recommended.

One particular iniquitous quirk of Cypriot car hire is the usual mandatory purchase, upon pick-up, of a full tank of petrol at grossly inflated rates, with the assumption that the car will be returned empty. Check terms and conditions carefully before booking online – often you can get a deal whereby you are only obliged to buy a half, or even quarter, tank up front. Sometimes you can agree on the spot to return the car full – the best option.

I'd like to hire a car **Tha íthela na nikiáso**
(tomorrow) **éna aftokínito (ávrio)**
for one day/a week **giá mía méra/mía evdomáda**
(international) driving licence **(diethnís) diploma**

CLIMATE

Cyprus enjoys sunny skies and low humidity almost all year round. On the coast, sea breezes temper the 32°C (90°F) heat of July and

August, but in Nicosia you can add 3–4 degrees on average, and the thermometer inland often goes above 37°C (99°F).

January through March see snowfalls in the Troödos mountain range – most seasons there is enough to permit skiing. The last few years have seen heavy rain between November and March, but there are plenty of fine days too, and the sea temperature remains just warm enough for swimming until New Year.

The following are average coastal temperatures:

		J	F	M	A	M	J	J	A	S	O	N	D
max	°C	17	17	19	23	26	30	32	33	31	27	22	18
	°F	63	63	66	73	79	86	90	91	88	81	72	64
min	°C	8	8	9	12	16	19	21	21	20	16	12	9
	°F	46	46	48	54	61	66	70	70	68	61	54	48

CLOTHING

In summer, wear comfortable, loose cotton clothing. July and August nights are very warm, but at other seasons they can be cool, so a light pullover is a good idea. In winter (late November to March), you'll need a raincoat or light winter coat, a warmer sweater or jacket, and warmer clothes.

On the beach, toplessness is widely tolerated; however, nudity in public is unacceptable accept at very remote coves. Informality is the general rule, but at posher hotels and restaurants people often dress up in the evening (and may be required to do so).

CRIME AND SAFETY

There is still so little crime on Cyprus that incidents which do take place make headlines, but burglary and car theft rates are rising. The island's only violence generally occurs in drunken brawls at Agia Napa. Otherwise, take the same precautions as you would at home.

D

DRIVING

Road conditions. Driving conditions are generally good in Cyprus, with well-surfaced, well-marked 'B' roads and fast motorways ('A') running along the south coast, linking Limassol, Larnaka, Agia Napa and Pafos, and heading inland to Nicosia. Beware of speeding, as there are regular radar-gun traps.

> Are we on the right road for ...? **Páme kalá giá ...?**
> left/right **aristerá/dexiá**
> Full tank, please. **Óso pérnei, parakaló**
>   /super/normal/diesel **soúper/aplí/dízel**
> My car has broken down. **I amáxi mou éhei páthi vlávi.**
> There's been an accident. **Égine éna atýhima.**

Main roads are paved and in good condition, and even many of the tertiary ('E') roads are easily negotiated. Short distances on minor ('F') roads, typically in the hills, can often be tackled in an ordinary car, but they are narrow (one-lane) and often unpaved, in addition to having steep, hairpin turns. A four-wheel-drive vehicle is best for the many rough tracks.

With the exception of the main roads between Nicosia and Keryneia, Morfou and Famagusta, the main coastal road east of Keryneia, and the main trunk road up the Karpasia Peninsula, roads in the North are often in poor condition.

In the cities traffic is fairly orderly. During the rush hour, expect traffic jams in Nicosia, Keryneia, Larnaka, Limassol and Pafos, especially leaving town in the early evening.

Rules and regulations. British and Irish motorists will feel at home in Cyprus, where traffic keeps to the left and roundabouts are frequent. Seat-belt use is compulsory in the front of cars and, where fitted, in the back, too. Drunk-driving control points are frequent at weekends and penalties stiff. Always carry your driving licence and car-hire documents with you.

Speed limits. The usual speed limits are 50kmh (30mph) in town and 100kmh (60mph) on motorways (lower limits may be posted).

Fuel. The price of petrol in Cyprus compares well with elsewhere in Europe – certainly less than in Greece, Italy, France or Britain. Diesel is cheaper, and it is possible to hire diesel cars. Filling stations generally close on Sundays and public holidays, but many have self-service fuel pumps that take cash or credit cards. They are plentiful in and around the main towns and resorts, but are rare in the mountains. If you're setting out on a back-country excursion, make sure the tank is full.

Parking. This is often difficult in Nicosia, Keryneia, Limassol, Pafos, Agia Napa and Larnaka. Fines are given for illegal parking. Try to find a meter or car park, or be willing to park in an uncontrolled residential area and walk a bit.

Problems. Call your hire company first. In an emergency, call the police (see emergency numbers, below).

Road signs. Most road signs, and most other signs imparting general information, use the standard international pictographs, and all written signs appear twice: once in Greek, once in English. In the North, signs are in Turkish and English.

E

ELECTRICITY

The standard current is 240 volts, 50 Hz ac; sockets are usually three-pin, as in the UK. Most hotels and some villas have 110-volt outlets for razors. Plug adaptors (*metaskhimatistés*), if necessary, may be provided free by hotels, or are available in bigger supermarkets and electrical merchants.

EMBASSIES AND CONSULATES

The following embassies and consulates are all in Southern Nicosia:

Australia: High Commission, Pindarou 27, Block A, Level 7; tel: 22753001, www.cyprus.embassy.gov.au

Canada: Honorary Consulate, Margarita House 402, Themistokli Dervi 15; tel: 22775508

Ireland: Embassy, Aianta 7; tel: 22818183, www.embassyofireland.com.cy

UK: High Commission, Alexandrou Palli; tel: 22861100, http://ukincyprus.fco.gov.uk/en

US: Embassy, Corner Metochiou and Ploutarchou, Egkomi; tel: 22393939, http://nicosia.usembassy.gov

EMERGENCIES

Republic of Cyprus:
Police, ambulance and fire brigade: **112**
Forest fires: **1407**
Northern Cyprus:
Police: **155;** ambulance: **112;** fire brigade: **199** forest fires **177**

G

GAY AND LESBIAN TRAVELLERS

Southern Cyprus has a small but growing gay and lesbian scene, and slowly improving acceptance of both the local gay and lesbian community and visitors from off-island. Gay Cyprus (www.gay-cyprus.com) has details on the local scene. Anther useful site is www.gay-cyprus.org. Northern Cyprus is considerably more conservative, but there's a summary of possibilities on www.turkeygay.net/cyprus.html.

GETTING THERE (see also Airports)

For most people, air travel is the only practical way of getting to Cyprus. Direct scheduled and charter flights link numerous British airports to Larnaka and Pafos. The flying time is around 4 hours 30 minutes. In addition to the many chartered airlines that fly to Cyprus, carriers with direct scheduled services from the UK include **Aegean Airlines** (www. aegeanair.com), **British Airways** (www.britishairways.com), **Cyprus Airways** (www.cyprusair.com.cy), **easyJet** (www.easyjet.com), **Jet 2** (www.jet2.com) and **Monarch** (www.monarch.co.uk).

Turkish airlines fly to Northern Cyprus from abroad via an intermediate stop in Turkey. Best of the carriers with service from England is **Pegasus** (www.flypgs.com) or **Turkish Airlines** (www. turkishairlines.com).

H

HEALTH AND MEDICAL CARE (see also Emergencies)

Medical treatment and assistance is offered free of charge to tourists in case of emergency, but it is recommended that you take out travel insurance to cover illness and accident while on holiday. Visitors from Britain, Ireland and other EU countries should bring along a European Health Insurance card (EHIC), which allows for free casualty ward medical treatment.

There are very capable doctors and dentists in the resorts, cities and larger towns, as well as good hospital facilities. Your hotel will advise you of the nearest English-speaking doctor. After-hours doctors are listed in local newspapers or can be contacted as follows: Nicosia, tel: 90901432; Agia Napa, tel: 90901433; Larnaka, tel: 90901434; Limassol, tel: 90901435; Pafos, tel: 90901436.

Stomach upsets should not be a problem, as hotels and restaurants observe high standards of cleanliness. Tap water is safe but often unpalatable; springs in the Troödos are much better. The sun can bronze, but also burn you. Take it in very small doses at first and use sunscreen.

A **pharmacy** (**farmakío**) is recognised by the sign outside – a red cross on a white background. They are open Monday–Friday 8am–1pm and 3 or 4–7pm (mornings only on Wednesday and Saturday). Certain pharmacies offer a 24-hour service – see local papers for listings.

Most medicines sold in the UK, US, Canada and Europe are available, but may require a prescription. Pharmacists can generally advise on minor ailments.

> Where's the nearest (all-night) pharmacy? **Pou íne to kondinótero farmakío pou efimerévei?**
> I need a doctor/dentist **Hriázome éna giatró/odontogiatró**
> …an ambulance **éna asthenofóro**
> … the hospital **to nosokomío**

L

LANGUAGE

English is spoken almost as a second language in all the resorts, and is understood by many people in Cyprus, both North and South. It is only well off the beaten track that a familiarity with Greek (in Southern Cyprus) or Turkish (in Northern Cyprus) is useful. If you do speak Greek or Turkish, be aware that the country dialects of each language spoken on Cyprus are almost incomprehensible to mainlanders, though educated people are taught, and use, 'proper' Greek/Turkish.

The table opposite lists the Greek alphabet with their capital and small forms, followed by the letter(s) to which they correspond in English. Below are a few phrases you might want to use:

> hello **yásoo (informal), yásas (formal)**
> good morning **kaliméra**
> good afternoon/evening **kalispéra**
> good night **kaliníkhta**
> please **parakaló**
> thank you **evharistó**
> yes **ne**
> no **óhi**

I don't speak Greek. **Den miló elliniká.**
I don't understand. Den katalavéno.
What does this mean? **Ti siméni aftó?**
Do you speak English? **Miláte angliká?**
excuse me **me sinhoríte**
where/when/how **pou/póte/pos**
yesterday/today/tomorrow **khthes/símera/ávrio**
big/small **megálo/mikró**
cheap/expensive **ftinó/akrivó**
open/closed **aniktó/klistó**
here/there **dó/ekí**
early/late **norís/argá**
How much is that? **Póso kánei aftó?**

Α	**α**	a	as in 'bar'
Β	**β**	v	as in 'veto'
Γ	**γ**	g	as in 'go' (before i- and e-sounds, pronounced like y in 'yes')
Δ	**δ**	d	like th in 'this'
Ε	**ε**	e	as in 'get'
Ζ	**ζ**	z	same as in English
Η	**η**	i	as in 'ski'
Θ	**θ**	th	as in 'thin'
Ι	**ι**	i	las in 'ski'
Κ	**κ**	k	same as in English
Λ	**λ**	l	same as in English
Μ	**μ**	m	same as in English
Ν	**ν**	n	same as in English
Ξ	**ξ**	x	as in 'box'
Ο	**ο**	o	as in 'road'
Π	**π**	p	in Cypriot, prounced as hard 'b'

P	ρ	r	same as in English
Σ	σ, ς	s	as in 'kiss'
T	τ	t	same as in English
Y	υ	y	as in 'country'
Φ	φ	f	same as in English
X	χ	ch, h	as in Scottish 'loch'
Ψ	ψ	ps	as in tipsy
O/Ω	ω	o	as in 'road'
AI	αι	e	as in hay
AY	αυ	av	as in avant-garde
EI	ει	i	as in ski
EY	ευ	ev	as in ever
OI	οι	i	as in ski
OY	ου	ou	as in soup
ΓΓ	γγ	ng	as in longer
ΓΚ	γκ	g	as in gone
ΓΞ	γξ	nx	as in anxious
ΜΠ	μπ	b or mb	as in beg or compass
ΝΤ	ντ	d or nd	as in dog or under

M

MAPS

The Cyprus Tourism Organisation provides a comprehensive island map and town plans of Nicosia, Limassol, Larnaka, Pafos, Agia Napa and Protaras, and their environs, plus the Troödos Mountains, free of charge. The best commercial town plans of the South are published by Selas.

I'd like a street plan of... **Tha íthela éna odikó hárti tis...**
a road map of this region **éna hárti aftís tis periochís**

MEDIA

Newspapers and magazines. There is a good selection of British and Irish newspapers and major American weekly news magazines available, sometimes a day after publication. The *Cyprus Mail*, an English-language daily (not Mon; www.cyprus-mail.com), has current news coverage and a good What's On section and weekly magazine. The *Cyprus Weekly* (also in English; www.incyprus.com.cy) carries lively features. In the North there's *Cyprus Today* (www.cyprustoday.net), an English weekly..

Radio and TV. The Cyprus Broadcasting Corporation (CyBC; www.cybc.com.cy) transmits English-language programmes from 6pm until midnight on its Second Programme. Radio BFBS (British Forces Broadcasting Service; www.bfbs.com) is on the air 24 hours a day, at various frequencies. Some hotels have BBC Radio Five Live. Multistar hotels offer cable and satellite television channels, including BBC World News, CNN and Sky. British sporting events can be watched on television in bars that subscribe to Sky Sports and/or the BBC.

MONEY

Currency. The euro is the national currency of Southern Cyprus. Cypriot euro coins have images of the indigenous moufflon sheep (1, 2 and 5 cents), the ancient Kyrenia ship (10, 20 and 50 cents), and the prehistoric idol of Pomos (€1 and €2). The euro banknotes are €5, €10, €20, €50, €100, €200 and €500.

In Northern Cyprus, the Turkish lira (TL) is the local currency. However, euros, pounds and dollars are accepted in hotels, restaurants and other businesses, albeit sometimes at a discount.

Banking. All banks, both South and North, are equipped with ATMs accepting foreign cards. Travellers's cheques are rarely accepted, or with great suspicion and delay, so are not worth the trouble. In the North, the best way to change euro or sterling into TL is at the numerous exchange (*döviz*) bureaux in Nicosia and Keryneia.

Credit cards. Major credit cards are welcome as payment by all car-hire firms, in most hotels and many, but not all, restaurants or shops.

> I want to change some pounds/dollars. **Thélo na alláxo**
> **merikés líres sterlínes/meriká dollária.**
> Can I pay with this credit card? **Boró na pliróso me aftí ti**
> **pistotikí kárta?**

O

OPENING HOURS

National museums and archaeological sites. These vary considerably, though always with very short hours on Sunday, if open at all. See individual citations in the Where to Go chapter.

Banks. Monday–Friday 8.15am–1.30pm May–Sept, otherwise Monday–Friday 8.30am–1.30pm and 3.15–4.45pm on Monday only.

Shops. From April to October, Southern shops are open Mon–Sat 8am–1pm and 4–7pm (closing half an hour later mid-summer). From November to March, shops open continuously Monday–Saturday 8.30am–6pm, but there are no afternoon hours on Wednesday and Saturday year-round. Northern schedules are similar: notionally in summer Monday–Saturday 8am–1.30pm, and Monday–Friday 2.30–6.30pm (not Wednesday); big supermarkets may open Sundays. In winter, expect opening Monday–Saturday 8am–6pm.

> Are you open tomorrow? **Íste aniktó ávrio?**

P

POLICE

The national police headquarters are off the Limassol-bound road in southeastern Nicosia, and there are divisional offices and stations in all main towns and resorts. Regular police officers in southern Cyprus wear blue uniforms and cruise around in blue-and-white police cars. Most members of the police (**Astynomía** in Greek; **Polis** in Turkish) speak some English. You'll recognise traffic policemen (common in Nicosia rush hours) by their white gloves and sleeves.

Where's the nearest police station? **Pou íne to kondinótero astynomikó tmíma?**

POST OFFICES

District Post Offices, of which there are three in Nicosia, two in Limassol, and one in both Larnaka and Pafos, are open Monday–Friday 7.30am–1.30pm and 3–6pm (3–5.30pm in July and August) and Saturday 9–11am. All other post offices are open Monday–Friday 7.30am–1.30pm, plus Wednesday 3–5.30pm (except July and August). Hours in the North are similar, if slightly longer on Saturday. Postboxes are coloured yellow in both the South and North.

Postage stamps may be bought at newsstands and kiosks. Postcards to Europe arrive within a week.

Where's the (nearest) post office? **Pou íne to kodinótero tahydromío?**
A stamp for this postcard, please. **Éna grammatósimo giaftín tin kartpostál, parakaló.**

PUBLIC HOLIDAYS

In addition to their own national holidays, Cypriots also celebrate certain Greek or Turkish holidays. Offices close on the following days. Shops remain open on some holidays: ask locally which ones. 'S' means in the South, 'N' means in the North.

1 Jan *Protohroniá* New Year's Day (S, N)

6 Jan *Theofánia* Epiphany (S)

25 Mar *Ikostipémptis Martíou (tou Evangelismoú)* Greek Independence Day (S)

1 Apr *Iméra Enárxeos Kypriakoú* Greek Cypriot National Day (S)

23 Apr National Sovereignty Day (N)

1 May *Protomagiá* Labour Day (S, N)

19 May Youth & Sport Day (N)

20 Jul Peace Operation Day (N)

1 Aug TMT Day (N)

15 Aug *Dekapendávgoustos (tis Panagías)* Dormition of the Virgin (S)

30 Aug Victory Day (N)

1 Oct *Iméra tis Anexartisías (tis Kýprou)* Cyprus Independence Day (S)

28 Oct *Ikostiogdóis Oktovríou ('Ohi')* 'No' Day, commemorating Greek defiance of Italian invasion of 1940 (S)

29 Oct Turkish Republic Day (N)

15 Nov TRNC Day (N)

25 Dec *Hristoúgenna* Christmas Day (S)

26 Dec *Sýnaxi tis Panagías* Gathering of the Virgin (S)

Movable dates:

Katharí Deftéra 1st Day of Lent/ (also known as Green or Clean Monday) (S)

Megáli Paraskeví Good Friday (S)

Deftéra tou Páskha Easter Monday (S)

Kataklysmós Pentecost (Festival of the Flood) (S)

Şeker Bayramı (N)

Mevlûd (N)

Kurban Bayramı (N)

R

RELIGION

You should dress modestly when visiting churches, monasteries and mosques. The dress code for monasteries is usually rigidly enforced and specifies long trousers for men, a below-the-knee skirt/dress for women and covered shoulders for both sexes. Churches are generally less formal. You must remove your shoes before entering a mosque.

T

TELEPHONE

To call Southern Cyprus from abroad, the international dialling code is 357; for the North it is 90. Area codes do not exist in southern Cyprus, merely eight-digit subscriber numbers. In Nicosia, they start with 22; Agia Napa 23; Larnaka 24; Limassol 25; Pafos 26. All mobiles begin with 9. The fixed-line area code for the entire North, which you use after 90, is 392; mobile codes are 533, 535, and 542. Northern subscriber numbers consist of seven digits; for land lines, omit 392 within the country, but you must use the codes when dialling mobiles. To make international calls from Cyprus, dial 00, then the country code.

Southern Cyprus has some of the cheapest mobile telephony in the world, such that public telephones are scarce and incurring surcharges by using hotel phones is folly. Even if you're only staying a week, it's well worth getting a pay-as-you-go SIM upon arrival. The two companies are CYTA-Vodaphone and MTN; CYTA-Vodaphone SIMs come with some talk time and are valid for 3 months – top it up once, and the number remains valid for a year. In the North, you'd do very well to get a local pay-as-you-go plan on local companies Türkcell or Telsim, as roaming with your home SIM is not subject to EU caps and bills can be shocking.

TIME ZONES

The chart below shows the time differences between Cyprus, which is on Eastern European Time (eet), and various cities in winter (UTC/GMT + 2 hours). In summer, clocks advance 1 hour, so the time difference with the UK and US stays the same.

New York	London	Cyprus	Jo'burg	Sydney	Auckland
5am	10am	noon	noon	9pm	11pm

TIPPING

Service charges are included in hotel and restaurant bills, but a little extra is always appreciated, especially for good service, to porters and chambermaids. Taxi drivers, hair stylists and tour guides all expect tips.

TOILETS

In the South, a few public toilets exist in parks of larger towns. Museums often have the cleanest facilities. In the North, pay toilets are conspicuous around old Nicosia, Keryneia harbour and Famagusta, but you'll prefer to use restaurant or hotel loos. They are indicated with the usual pictographs.

Where are the toilets? **Pou íne ta apohoritíria?**

TOURIST INFORMATION

The **Cyprus Tourism Organisation**, or CTO **(Kypriakós Organismós Tourismoú – KOT**; www.visitcyprus.com), which covers the **South**, is a mine of information, with free brochures and maps.
UK: 17 Hanover Street, London, W1S 1YP; tel: (020) 7569 8800
US: 13 E 40th Street, New York, NY 10016; tel: (212) 683-5280; www.visitcyprus.com

In Cyprus, the CTO maintains offices at **Larnaka Airport** arrivals, at **Pafos Airport** arrivals, at **Limassol harbour** cruise ship terminal, and in the following major tourist centres: Nicosia old town (marked on our map), Limassol centre (marked on map) and Potamos Germasogeias tourist strip, Larnaka, Pafos (marked on map), Agia Napa, Polis, Pano Platres, and Paralimni.

For information on **Northern Cyprus:**

UK: 29 Bedford Square, London, WC1B 3EO; tel: (020) 7631 1930; www.simplynorthcyprus.com.

US: 1667 K Street, Suite 690, Washington DC, 20006; tel: (202) 887 6198

In Northern Cyprus, there are tourist offices in **Keryneia/Girne** on the old port, **Famagusta/Gazimağusa** old town by the Land Gate, and **Nicosia/Lefkoşa** in the Keryneia/Girne Gate.

TRANSPORT

Cyprus has no railways and the inter-urban bus service is not always frequent, especially on Sundays or to/from remote villages – just one or two departures per day, if that. Bus services within the towns and resorts, however, are good. Private and shared taxis fill the public transport gap.

Private taxis. Vehicles are metered. You can hail a taxi on the street or call for one by telephone.

Shared service taxis. In the South, service taxis (actually minibuses) take from four to eight passengers and connect all major towns every half-hour. The main nationwide company is Travel & Express, fares and booking on tel: 77777474 or www.travelexpress.com.cy. Prices are fixed and quite reasonable. In the North, minibuses called **dolmuş** operate between the towns but only depart when they are full.

> Where can I get a taxi/service taxi/minibus? **Pou boró na vro éna taxí/yperastiká taxi?**

VISAS AND ENTRY REQUIREMENTS

Entering the Republic. Nationals of the EU, Australia, Canada, Japan, New Zealand, Singapore, the US and some other countries can stay in Cyprus for up to three months without a visa. Legal points of entry are the ports of Larnaka, Limassol and Pafos, and the international airports of Larnaka and Pafos.

Entering the North. Visitors travelling via Ercan Airport or the ports of Famagusta (Gazimağusa) or Keryneia (Girne) in Turkish-controlled Northern Cyprus, and who are citizens of EU states, may cross freely in both directions between North and South at the official crossing points. Other nationals can expect trouble – including denial of entry – trying to enter the South from the North, even if no entry stamp for the North is actually recorded in their passport. Note that the regulations and their implementation may change frequently and without notice.

WEBSITES AND INTERNET ACCESS

www.cyprusevents.net One-stop what's-on resource for southern concerts, theatre, cinema.

www.mcw.gov.cy/mcw/DA/DA.nsf/DMLmuseums_en/DML museums_en?OpenDocument All the museums, archaeological sites and antiquities issues in the South.

www.cyprus-conflict.net Outstanding, impartial overview of how the island got to where it is now.

www.cyprus-weather.org The best local forecast site.

www.hamamboculeri.org Best contrarian blog-site on the island, with both Turkish-Cypriots and Greek-Cypriots; many English articles.

www.northcyprusonline.com Tourism site covering the North.

www.unficyp.org The UN force's site; much more interesting than it sounds.

www.windowoncyprus.com Good general site covering the South.

Free WiFi zones are common in the South, typically in bars or cafés or the common areas of hotels; WiFi in rooms may be charged for, exorbitantly. The North is somewhat behind in this respect, but improving.

Recommended Hotels

Most Cypriot hotels are self-contained resorts aimed at package clients; there are relatively few small inns with unique character.

Mega-hotels dominate the southern coastline, but there are some foothill inns of great charm. Pafos district has the widest choice, from beachfront hotels to wonderful inland retreats. South Nicosia has a good range of hotels, but accommodation choice in the Troödos Mountains is limited.

Northern Cypriot hotels can be noticeably cheaper than their Southern counterparts, but many are marred by the casino trade. Most accommodation is in and around Keryneia, but there are also good if modest options on the Karpasia Peninsula.

€€€€	over 200 euros
€€€	150–200 euros
€€	100–150 euros
€	under 100 euros

SOUTHERN CYPRUS

NICOSIA

Almond Business Suites €€ *Ikostipemptis Martiou 11, new town tel: 22879131, www.almond-businesshotel.com*. Self-catering one-bedroom apartments with contemporary furnishings, popular not only with business people. Quiet location and free WiFi are other pluses.

Centrum €–€€ *Pasikratous 15, Laïki Geitonia, tel: 22456444, www.centrumhotel.net*. Nicosia's only salubrious budget option, this was redone since 2010. Rooms are often quirkily laid out. Fast, free WiFi, friendly staff and an atmospheric adjacent restaurant for breakfast.

Classic €€ *Rigainis 94, tel: 22664006, www.classic.com.cy*. Overhauled in 2011, this has small, tastefully furnished rooms, good breakfasts, an on-site restaurant, garden bar and a well-equipped gym. The best-value old-town choice, with helpful staff.

Cleopatra €€ *Florinis 8, new town, tel: 22844000, www.cleopatra. com.cy.* Comfortable hotel, popular with foreign businessmen, as well as tourists with cars (some private parking). Rooms in three grades have been redone since 2009, with butler sinks and rain showers in the baths, neutral or 'Bordello Baroque' décor in the sleeping areas. Common facilities include a large outdoor pool, fitness centre, good-value lobby bistro, and full-service poolside eatery.

LARNAKA AND REGION

Cyprus Villages Traditional Houses € *Tochni and Kalavasos, tel: 24332998, www.cyprusvillages.com.cy.* A dozen converted buildings in these two villages were among the first (1980s) restoration projects, and still among the best. They range from apartments by the Tochni reception office, with central heating and down duvets for winter, to self-contained traditional houses with private pools. Best to arrange all-inclusive packages directly with them.

The Library €€ *Central Kalavasos, tel: 24817071, www.libraryhotel cyprus.com.* This dusty old inn was impeccably restored in 2010 as a 'Wellness Retreat' with a state-of-the-art spa as centrepiece, and, yes, a well-stocked library on the ground floor. No expense has been spared in appointing the units (including three suites), breakfast is copious, and there's a good restaurant on site.

Palm Beach Hotel and Bungalows €€€ *Larnaka–Dekeleia road, tel: 24846600, www.palmbeachotel.com.* Plenty of palm trees indeed in the lush gardens abutting hard-packed Oroklini beach; half the somewhat dated standard rooms overlook this. Viewless garden bungalows have a higher standard, though this hotel's four stars derive from common facilities like gym/sauna, watersports and service levels.

AGIA NAPA

Alion Beach €€ *Kryou Nerou, tel: 23722900, www.alion.com.* Much the best value five-star hotel hereabouts, built on a smallish scale, with helpful staff and scrumptious breakfasts taken out on a terrace. Rooms (prefer sea view) are large, with clean, unfussy decor; bathrooms have proper shower screens. Pools, both indoor and out, are a bit of a joke but who cares when an excellent beach is five steps distant.

Napa Mermaid €€€ *Kryou Nerou 45, tel: 23721606, www.napa mermaidhotel.com*. This formerly dull high-rise got a makeover in 2007 to emerge as a designer hotel with switched-on staff. Best of the four room types are the junior suites, with big balconies and plush furnishings; the grand suites are effectively two-bedroom apartments with a jacuzzi on the terrace. Pool, tennis court, gym on site.

So Nice Boutique Suites €€ *Leoforos Nissi 103, tel: 23723010, www.sonice.com.cy*. Design-led bungalow suites with an arresting colour palette just inland from peaceful Landa cove; prefer senior grade rooms, which accommodate four and have a roof terrace. There's a poolside restaurant and elevated sushi bar (summer only). Big pool, wedding area on lawn, but no gym or spa.

LIMASSOL (LEMESOS) AND REGION

Columbia Beach Resort €€€€ *Pissouri Bay, tel: 25833000, www. columbia-hotels.com*. This family-friendly hotel shares a sybaritic spa with its adjacent affiliate, the Columbia Beach Hotel, but is closer to the excellent beach (beyond lush gardens). Large suites in three grades (including family), arrayed around an enormous lagoon pool, have stone, wood and tropical touches.

Four Seasons €€€€ *B6 coast road, 9km (5.5 miles) east of town, tel: 25858000, www.fourseasons.com.cy*. The best self-contained resort on Cyprus, where you get what you pay for, with consistently excellent service. The dominant motif is oasis, with a jungly atrium and koi ponds. From a range of units, the adults-only garden suites and the family quads behind the beach are remarkable. Amenities include three pools, spa, gym and on-site scuba school. Three in-house restaurants are among the best in Limassol, with considerable walk-in trade.

Lofou Agrovino € *Lofou village centre, tel: 25470202, www.lofou-agrovino.com*. One of the top agrotourism projects, in a showcase village, these studios have been meticulously renovated from old houses or purpose-built. There are fireplaces or wood stoves for winter, clothes washers, and full kitchens with dishwashers. Eat at owner Kostas' co-run, *mezé* format *Lofou Taverna*, while breakfast is served in a separate café-wine bar.

Londa €€€ *Georgiou tou Protou, 5km (3 miles) east of town, tel: 25865555, www.londahotel.com.* The city's first and still best boutique hotel, with crisp lines and white, beige and wood tones lending a vaguely Asian feel to variable rooms and suites. Popular with local and foreign trendies, who pack out the in-house restaurant and lobby bar at weekends. Good service from smart, young, international staff. Excellent spa, small beach with water sports, decent pool.

TROÖDOS MOUNTAINS

Linos Inn € *Palaia Kakopetria, tel: 22923161, www.linos-inn.com.cy.* Antique-furnished rooms, studios and suites occupy a group of restored, linked old village houses – a romantic weekend getaway popular with Cypriots as well as foreigners. Some have river-view terraces and fireplaces. Popular bar, with live music at weekends, and a busy restaurant.

Semiramis € *Spyrou Kyprianou 55, Pano Platres, tel: 25422777, www. semiramishotelcyprus.com.* This carefully refurbished 1920s mansion is now Platres' most distinctive hotel. Rooms have a preponderance of double beds, solid wood floors, fanlights over the windows, modern baths and occasional balconies. You take breakfast in the ground-floor salon or out on the terrace; half-board is available at the competent, co-managed Village Restaurant.

PAFOS AND REGION

Alexander the Great €€€ *Leoforos Poseidonos, Kato Pafos, tel: 26965000 www.kanikahotels.com.* One of the less pretentious Pafos hotels overlooks a small sandy cove. Adults-only garden cabanas have veneer floors, plunge pools or patios, and fully modernised bathrooms; main wing rooms were refurbished to the same standard in early 2013. An unusually large indoor pool, pleasant spa, and three on-site restaurants remain the same.

Almyra €€€€ *Leoforos Poseidonos, Kato Pafos, tel: 26888700, www. thanoshotels.com.* The oldest hotel in Kato Pafos was renovated during 2003–8 in minimalist boutique style, popular equally with families and trendy couples, lodged in separate wings (and with separate pools). The best units are the adult Aethon rooms and the Kyma suites with lawn terraces. The spa has a stunning sea view. Three varied restaurants are sensibly priced for the hotel's category.

Aphrodite Beach € *Asprokremos Beach, tel: 26321001, www.aphrodite-beachhotel.com.* The rooms here are resolutely 1980s style, but that's forgiven when you consider the warm welcome from the multilingual owners, the excellent meals available, and a position immediately above the best beach in Pafos district. Products of the adjacent orchards find their way into the food (half-board recommended).

Ayii Anargyri Natural Healing Spa €€€–€€€€ *Miliou village tel: 26814000, www.aasparesort.com.* Occupying the site of a nondescript monastery (only the church remains), this retreat in a lush stream valley has the most striking spa in Cyprus, sumptuous breakfasts and vast common areas. The best units are the hillside garden bungalows, with solid wood furniture and some private jacuzzis, or the ''monks' rooms' with exposed stonework, huge beds and spring water on tap.

Lasa Heights € *Lasa village outskirts, tel: 26732777, www.lasaheights. com.* The nucleus of this country inn is the helpful owner's grandfather's former coffee shop, now the breakfast area. It's an airy spot with sweeping views from Pafos to Polis, ideal for mountain-bikers and wildlife-spotters. The best, antique-furnished room is in the old stone building; others, in the new wing, are contemporary, with modern baths and pastel colour accents.

Paradisos Hills € *1km (0.5 miles) east of Lysos village, tel: 26322287, www.paradisoshills.com.* A stone-clad country hotel, set as per the name, run by two South African-Cypriot sisters. Large, tasteful, balconied rooms have solid-wood furnishings and mostly sweeping sea or mountain views. Food is good, with the Sunday buffet a local institution. Common area décor is rustic without veering into kitsch; there's a large, wind-protected pool on a lower terrace.

Thalassa €€€–€€€€ *Coral Bay, 11km (7 miles) from Pafos, tel: 26623222, www.thalassa.com.cy.* This mostly suite hotel is known for its top-notch spa and personal butler service. One-bedroom suites are large, with long balconies (looking to either sunrise or sunset) and quality furnishings including sound/DVD systems. There are two restaurants, a large pool and steps down to the beach – or a private lido.

NORTHERN CYPRUS

KERYNEIA (GIRNE) AND REGION

Bellapais Gardens €€ *Beylerbeyi (Bellapais) village centre, tel: (392) 815 6066, www.bellapaisgardens.com.* The management here could just let the location sell things; instead they offer top-drawer service, an excellent restaurant (with significant walk-in trade, plus the best breakfast in the North) and high-standard chalet units, last redone in 2010. The views, from the restaurant or spring-fed pool, are to die for.

The Hideaway Club €€ *Trimithi (Edremit) village centre, tel: (392) 822 2620, www.hideawayclub.com.* The returned London-Cypriot owners and their staff have an almost telepathic knack for anticipating guests' needs. Rooms/suites in several grades aren't bad either, all with complimentary bath robes, iron bedsteads, throw rugs and hammocks. Poolside bar/restaurant is the heart of the 'club'.

Pia Bella €–€€ *Iskenderun Cad 14, east Keryneia, tel: (392) 815 5321, www.piabella.com.* A somewhat grim location is belied once inside this lushly landscaped complex, with two pools, one for serious swimming. The two rear wings, with their 'superior' rooms, suites and self-catering units, are preferable to the main building. Assiduous service ensures a loyal, largely Brit, clientele.

KARPASIA (KARPAZ)

Karpaz Arch Houses € *North neighbourhood, Dipkarpaz (Rizokarpazo), tel: (392) 372 2009, www.karpazarchhouses.com.* The most successful restoration scheme in the North incorporates many soaring traditional arches – thus the name. The best units are next to the restaurant.

INDEX

Berlitz pocket guide

Cyprus

Ninth Edition 2013

Written by Paul Murphy
Updated by Marc Dubin
Edited by Tom Stainer
Art Editor: Shahid Mahmood
Series Editor: Tom Stainer
Production: Tynan Dean and Rebeka Ellam

Printed in China by CTPS

Berlitz Trademark Reg. U.S. Patent Office and other countries. Marca Registrada. Used under licence from the Berlitz Investment Corporation

Photography credits: Caroline Jones/Apa Publications 2/3T, 2/3M, 2/3M, 2/3M, 2/3M, 4/5T, 6TL, 6ML, 7MC, 7MC, 7TC, 12, 15, 18/19, 20, 28, 34, 34/35, 40, 43, 44, 50, 53, 54/55, 56/57, 58, 59, 60, 60/61, 64, 67, 71, 72, 73, 76, 78, 85, 88, 90, 94, 96, 98/99; George Taylor/Apa Publications 2TL, 2TC, 3TC, 22, 32, 39, 41, 42, 49, 66, 74/75, 80, 82, 84, 103; 83; Dreamstime.com 87; Bill Wassman/Apa Publications 100; Britta Jaschinski/Apa Publications 5MC; iStockphoto 4/5M, 4ML, 4TL; 46;, Jon Davidson/Apa Publications 24, 36; Paul Murphy/Apa Publications 2MC, 6ML, 8, 10, 17, 38, 48, 54, 62, 68, 93, 104/105; Paul Phillips 70; Richard Nowitz/Apa Publications 4TL, 5TC

Cover picture: Spila Riccardo/SIME-4Corners Images

Every effort has been made to provide accurate information in this publication, but changes are inevitable. The publisher cannot be responsible for any resulting loss, inconvenience or injury.

Contact us

At Berlitz we strive to keep our guides as accurate and up to date as possible, but if you find anything that has changed, or if you have any suggestions on ways to improve this guide, then we would be delighted to hear from you.

Berlitz Publishing, PO Box 7910,
London SE1 1WE, England.
email: berlitz@apaguide.co.uk
www.insightguides.com/berlitz